# FIT TO PRINT

2/01  IA - NY

# FIT TO PRINT

## The Canadian Student's Guide to Essay Writing

### JOANNE BUCKLEY

McMaster University

HARCOURT
BRACE
CANADA

**Harcourt Brace & Company, Canada**

Toronto  Montreal  Fort Worth  New York  Orlando
Philadelphia  San Diego  London  Sydney  Tokyo

**Canadian Cataloguing in Publication Data**

Buckley, Joanne, 1953-
  Fit to print: the Canadian student's guide to essay writing

4th ed.
Includes index.

ISBN 0-7747-3585-6

1. Report writing.  2. Exposition (Rhetoric).
I. Title.

LB2369.B83 1997      808'.042      C97-930679-5

Acquisitions Editor: Kelly V. Cochrane
Senior Developmental Editor: Laura Paterson Pratt
Production Editor: Louisa Schulz
Production Co-ordinator: Carolyn McLarty
Copy Editor: Beverley Beetham Endersby
Cover Design: Sonya V. Thursby/Opus House
Interior Design: Jack Steiner Graphic Design
Typesetting and Assembly: Bookman Typesetting Co.
Printing and Binding: Best Book Manufacturers, Inc.

This book was printed in Canada.

    3   4   5     02   01   00   99

## Other Titles Available in the

# ■ Harbrace Guides to Student Success Series

"*Career Success* is a practical, positive, and useful guide for anyone who is seeking a fulfilling career. High school students, college students, and adults looking for a career change will all benefit from the practical advice and encouragement that the author gives."

Lindsay Holmes
Student
University of Calgary

"*Fit to Print* takes a clear, concise, no-nonsense approach to the problems of essay writing. Students (especially first-year students) will be able to understand this compact text and will not have to wade through it — as is the case with so many discursive composition books."

William Benzie
Professor
University of Victoria

"For its emphasis on well-written prose and its easy-to-follow, practical approach, *Fit to Print* is an invaluable aid for student writers in any discipline. Few books offer so much practical information to change student writing from a struggle to a success."

Jim McDonald and Karen Jacob
Instructors
Humber College

"*Fit to Print* is the book I used most during my first three weeks at school. Returning to school after twelve years, I found this to be the most helpful of all my textbooks in real practical terms. I would highly recommend this book for anyone just entering college or returning to school after having been away from the classroom for some time."

David Beattie
Student
Sir Sandford Fleming College

"For students who want to improve their study skills *Learning for Success* is an excellent resource. It explains the theory of study skills in understandable language, gives examples, and asks for student response."

Carol Potter
Instructor
Dawson College

"*Learning for Success* is an excellent, practical guide for students in college and university, as well as senior high school level. It is a great resource for beginning counsellors, as it provides valuable information on various topics related to student success."

Irmo Marini
Counselling Co-ordinator
Lakehead University

"Over the summer I read the whole thing and in my second year I used *Success in Social Sciences* in every subject. This book is not written in textbook terms; the examples are as if you took them off my exams, and I learned something new on every page. Your book and its information will stay with me throughout all my school years!"

Corrie Godsmark
Okanagan University College

"Who is this person? Can I meet them and shake their hand? The nail was hit on the head **so** many times, I think we've built a house! *Transitions: Succeeding in College and University* is very realistic, down to earth, and it centres around you the individual. I can't stress how realistic it is; it's so refreshing."

Joanne Cheverie
Student
University of Prince Edward Island

"*Making Your Mark* reflects a lot of current experience working with students. The writing is precise, direct, and invites one to keep reading. It is consistent and very clear."

Joan Fleet
Counselling and Career Development Services
University of Western Ontario

# Preface

The fourth edition of *Fit to Print*, like its predecessors, is intended for students grappling with the problems of writing, in general, and of essays, in particular. Used in a university, college, or secondary school environment, *Fit to Print* can be either the principal textbook in a composition course or an inexpensive supplementary guide in the humanities or social sciences. As previous editions have done, the book examines the multiple forms of the essay, both expository and persuasive, including the research essay, the essay exam, the analytic book review, the précis, and the literary essay. To assist both teachers in the classroom and students working on their own with the text, answers to some of the exercises are now included at the back of the book, and the instructor's manual contains even more exercises.

Like the earlier editions, this one gives students sound advice on the organization of the essay, and on specific questions of grammar and style; reviewers have suggested some substantial improvements, which have now been incorporated:

1. More and updated information on APA and MLA documentation, including advice on how to list electronic sources, such as CD-ROMs and on-line material
2. More information on manuscript preparation, eliminating the need for separate style sheets
3. Improved organization of chapters
4. New exercises on matters of composition, grammar, and style
5. Answers in the text
6. An instructor's guide with extra materials for practice and testing.

This new edition of *Fit to Print* maintains certain features that have been approved by teachers across the country:

1. The text takes the student through the writing process, from invention to final proofreading, so that students can work on both organization and craftsmanship.
2. The lessons and exercises are clear and readable, and they deal with specific grammatical and stylistic concerns.
3. MLA, APA, and University of Chicago styles of documentation are all covered in detail.
4. The examples draw on Canadian subject matter.
5. The tone is friendly and accessible.
6. The book uses genuine student examples, and essay assignments across disciplines.
7. The book can be used both as a classroom text and as a self-help guide.

# ■ Acknowledgements

*Fit to Print*, Fourth Edition, is the result of lots of support and assistance from friends and colleagues. I would especially like to thank Kelly Cochrane and Laura Paterson Pratt of Harcourt Brace & Company, Canada, as well as the reviewers who made thoughtful suggestions for the text's improvement — Susan J. Brown, Wilfrid Laurier University; Barry McKinnon, The College of New Caledonia; amd Nicholas Tavuchis, University of Manitoba . Thanks also go to students who permitted me to use their work, and to Karen Nelles, for testing some of the exercises for me. Kathleen Fraser and Marie Davis were unfailingly kind and helpful. Special thanks are due to Kevin Hutchings, who was a gifted and tireless research assistant on my behalf. My new colleagues at McMaster University, especially Geoffrey Rockwell, were terrific for my morale. David Gates kept me laughing; Mary Buckley kept me living well. Despite the jokes, the book is still not called *Fit to Be Tied*.

## About the Harbrace Guides to Student Success Series

A series of accessible, affordable, and practical books, the Harbrace Guides to Student Success are dedicated to fostering student success in all its diversity. Look for forthcoming titles on conducting a job search, writing research papers, and writing for the social sciences.

## A Note from the Publisher

Thank you for selecting *Fit to Print: The Canadian Student's Guide to Essay Writing*, Fourth Edition, by Joanne Buckley. The author and publisher have devoted considerable time to the careful development of this book. We appreciate your recognition of this effort and accomplishment.

We want to hear what you think about *Fit to Print: The Canadian Student's Guide to Essay Writing*. Please take a few minutes to fill in the stamped reader reply card at the back of the book. Your comments and suggestions will be valuable to us as we prepare new editions and other books.

# Contents

# Introduction— Defining the Essay

> The essay is a literary device for saying almost everything about almost anything.
>
> *Aldous Huxley*

## ■ If at First You Don't Succeed . . .

The essay, as any dictionary will tell you, is an attempt. This definition itself ought to be reassuring if you have ever worried about how you would be able to write an essay. You can't fail as long as what you write is a sincere attempt to come to terms with a particular subject. The finished essay succeeds insofar as it is an honest attempt to elucidate some aspect of your topic.

An essay need not fail as long as your ideas are treated fairly, honestly, and in a spirit of thorough and intensive investigation — and you have communicated these ideas to the reader! If the essay seems an especially burdensome assignment, it may be because most of us are not accustomed to independent thought. Try to think of the essay as an opportunity to stretch your intellectual muscles and to think your own thoughts.

To write an essay is to engage in a creative process, to bring an idea to life. The essay itself, however, is a finished product, not a record of the process by which you wrote it.

Whether you are writing an expository essay (meant to explain something), or a persuasive essay (meant to argue something), the essay's chief purpose is to present a thesis that focusses your ideas and conveys them to the reader in a way that shows their worth and their validity. Depending on the occasion, an essay may be formal or informal; however, academic writing usually demands formality. Depending on the nature of the assignment, the essay may be a product of reasoning or of a combination of reasoning and research.

This text deals both with the essentials of essay writing and with the variations expected in different kinds of assignments. Skim its contents first to acquaint yourself with the most important steps of essay writing. If you are unfamiliar with the basic requirements of the essay, pay special attention to Parts One, Two, and Three. If you are unsure of the specific guidelines for a particular kind of essay, check the pertinent section in Part Four. Then, as you write your next essay, use this book as a step-by-step guide. It will provide helpful suggestions on how to organize your thinking, and how to present your material in the most effective manner.

Remember that the essay is an attempt to think through your ideas in a structured way. Each attempt will teach you more about how the process works for you.

# ■ Try, Try Again

As you plan and write the essay, you will be trying various ideas on for size. The process of writing an essay involves finding some part of a large topic that fits your attitude toward and interest in the subject. Compromise is essential. The essay must fit both you and the topic: it will show you and the reader what you know and what you have yet to learn. For best results, choose a topic in which you have some personal stake. Make sure that you can treat the topic satisfactorily within the required word limit and within the time constraints of the assignment.

# ■ Overcoming Your Fears

Writing is hard work, even for those who choose to write for a living, as a glance at some of the epigraphs that begin each chapter of this book may well illustrate. You may find it difficult to get your thoughts down on paper, or even to feel that you have any important thoughts to record. Here is some advice meant to make starting to write easier.

1. **Divide the writing process into smaller steps; don't try to do everything at once.**

   Look again at the table of contents in this book. It should suggest to you that your first task is finding some central focus; your next task, building an outline; your third task, writing a preliminary draft; and your final task, revising the whole. Don't skip any of these steps.

2. **Don't ignore your real questions about a topic because you feel they betray your ignorance.**

   The essay is meant to be an exploration of something; if you knew everything about the subject before you began, you wouldn't need to write. In large part, the writing process is meant to help you and your reader discover something.

3. **Pay attention to your real interests in and your real objections to the subject matter.**

   Let the focus of your conversations and your wondering become the focus of your essay.

4. **Don't approach the assignment in a perfunctory manner.**

   Ask yourself why the assignment is a good one and what connections it makes with the course, or with other courses, or with other things you have read.

### 5. Don't expect too much from an essay.

An essay is not meant to provide a definitive answer; instead, it explores what you think, and why you think it, in as clear a way as possible.

### 6. Gather information and ideas and write them down as you go along.

### 7. Ask questions of your instructor and seek his or her help with the delineation of your topic.

### 8. Try not to think of your instructor as an enemy, seeking to trip you up.

Think of your reader as someone engaged in the topic and deeply interested in your point of view.

### 9. Explain your ideas to a friend; the transition to paper should involve little more than careful documentation and editing.

### 10. Learn from your mistakes.

Diagnose what went wrong with previous assignments and resolve not to make the same mistakes again.

# PART ONE

# Developing the Essay

# Devising a Thesis

> Writing is just having a sheet of paper, a pen, and not a shadow of an idea of what you're going to say.
>
> *Françoise Sagan*

Usually when you begin to write an essay, you will have in mind a broad area of concentration or a fundamental topic that you mean to explore. To write a successful essay, you must find the focal point of your discussion — the centre of your thought, from which the points you make may radiate outward. This focal point is the thesis statement.

Topics are only the starting point for your thinking. They tell you only the general area of investigation. Whether you are given a topic by the instructor or you find your own, the topic must be narrowed down to serve as the focus of your paper. Like the bull's eye in the middle of a dartboard, the thesis statement is the centre that holds your argument together. An essay succeeds because the point to be made is directly on target, and the significance of the point is firmly established.

## ■ Discovering a Topic

If your instructor has not suggested areas for exploration, you will have to create your own, usually subject to his or her approval. This process need not be drudgery; it gives you the opportunity to explore your own interest in the subject.

The following are some suggestions for finding a general topic or area of interest:

1. Skim the index and table of contents of any book mentioned in class as a useful source.
2. Skim through class notes and text for ideas that catch your imagination.
3. Ask questions about the meaning and value of the subject.
4. Look at class assignments and essay questions and ask yourself what their point is. Why are these questions particularly fitting to the subject area you are dealing with?
5. Listen to yourself. What issues and matters of concern come up in your conversations outside of class?
6. Allow yourself the chance to express your real puzzlement about something you have read. If you don't understand something crucial in your

area of study, make finding out more about it one of the goals of your investigation.

Always write down ideas as you go along.

## ■ Shopping for a Thesis Statement

Often, you will be given a general topic and be instructed to narrow it down. Remember, though, a topic is only a general idea in need of development. Suppose you were asked in an Administrative Studies course to write an essay of 2500–3000 words about productivity growth in Japan. Obviously, this is a broad subject that could yield several promising thesis statements. By itself, however, it is just a phrase and makes no meaningful statement. Keep this example in mind as you read through the following tips on developing a specific thesis statement.

### Consider the writing situation

When you develop a topic, keep these determining factors in mind:

1.  your interests, strengths, and weaknesses
2.  the reader's expectations
3.  the restrictions of the assignment

### Use whatever you have at your disposal

1.  supplemental bibliographies you may have been given
2.  advice from the instructor
3.  material from the course itself
4.  your native wit
5.  library materials — books, journals, and audio-visual materials
6.  the Internet

### Ask questions about the general topic

Your first question with regard to our sample topic might be "What about it?" Your sources, both in class and out, may have revealed to you that Japanese productivity growth has greatly surpassed that of Canada since World War II.

Your next question might be "Why?" suggesting a cause-and-effect development, or even "How?" suggesting an argument based on classification (the breakdown of ideas into categories) or on process (the orderly presentation of steps). Refer also to Chapter 5 for some suggested approaches to topic development.

### Consider your topic in conjunction with something else

Try joining your topic to these conjunctions: "and," "or," "but," "so." These linking words should give you some idea of what might be productively attached to your topic to yield interesting results.

"And," for example, might help you think of things that can be compared (or contrasted) with your subject: Japanese productivity and Canadian productivity, for instance.

"Or" might lead you to consider a controversy about the causes of Japanese productivity: advanced technology or employee motivation, for example.

"But" might allow you to refute the position of a particular authority on the subject, or to prove that the rate of productivity growth in Japan's case is more a result of the stage of its industrial development than of superior technology or administration.

### Consider key words that form part of the topic

Ask yourself about the nuances of the question or topic for discussion: is there ambiguity or potential for development in the wording of the question? When setting questions, instructors usually have only a sketchy idea in mind; try to see in the topic as much as or more than they have.

In our sample general topic, one word to which this tactic might apply is "productivity." To develop your topic, you might investigate what particular areas are most productive, to find a clue for your response. You might also want to explore exactly what is meant by "growth." Does it mean increased profits, expansion in number of products, or development of new products?

### Consult your own taste

Your taste in topics should be consulted before you settle on anything. About the only serious mistake you can make is to choose a topic simply because it looks easier than the others. A challenge is often the best choice since it allows you to ponder the topic rather than assuming, probably incorrectly, that the main point is clear or the answer obvious.

### Try on the topic before you decide

Always play with the topic before you work on it. Play with ideas by scratching them down haphazardly on a sheet of paper without regard (for now) to problems of order or clarity. This kind of unstructured thinking will open up the possibilities of the question or the topic for you in a way that no amount of tidy compartmentalizing can.

### Brainstorm by writing ideas down

1.  Try clustering ideas together according to their associations for you.
2.  Try drawing diagrams, connecting various ideas.
3.  Check the meanings of words in the topic, and perhaps even their etymologies, for clues to the direction you should take.

## ■ A Working Thesis vs. a Polished Thesis Statement

If you follow the guidelines above, you should be able to arrive at a narrow focus for your paper. But even a thesis statement should be subject to revision. Because it is normally part of the introduction to a paper, writers often mistakenly assume that it should be written first. In fact, your real thesis statement may emerge only after you have made several false starts.

Since you have to start somewhere, begin with a working thesis. It will allow you to consider your material from a tentative point of view. If you find that the evidence begins to contradict it, or you no longer consider it the centre of your discussion, redefine your statement to suit the new circumstances.

The thesis statement that appears in your finished introduction will be the best description of what you are trying to prove and of how you propose to do it. For example, your thesis statement on the subject of Japanese productivity growth might look like this:

> *The enormous increase recorded in productivity growth in Japan in the past ten years is largely the result of new theories of employee relations that have been developed in Japanese industry.*

### Look before you leap

Once you have formulated a contention, that is, some idea of what your approach to the topic is going to be, you must formulate a thesis statement, along with some sense of the essay's ultimate direction. You may want to visit the library to take note of what relevant books and journal articles are available on your specific subject, and of whether they support or contradict your working thesis.

To write a good thesis statement, you need to remember that a strong thesis is a contention that forms the basis of your argument. It is what you are trying to show the reader. A good thesis statement takes into account the purpose of the writing and its audience, but it does more than that. For instance, your purpose might be to define for a beginner the perfect golf swing. Although this idea shows promise, it is not a thesis statement. To transform it, you need to make a claim. Look at this statement:

> *A perfect golf swing demands a proper grip, delicate balance, and excellent timing.*

It is a strong thesis statement because it makes a claim that the rest of the essay, presumably, will go on to support.

Suppose, now, that your topic is "learning a foreign language." Your purpose is to tell your reader what you consider the best way to learn a language. You must not, however, leave the topic too vague. Instead, you might compose a thesis statement like the following:

> *The best way to learn a foreign language is through active practice and immersion among native speakers.*

This thesis is stronger than, say, one that argues that learning a foreign language is difficult, because this one is contentious: some might, after all, disagree and claim that study and reading are more important than practice and immersion. It is your job to make your case convincingly.

##   What to Look for in a Thesis Statement

### Personal conviction

No writing of any power is ever possible without commitment to the subject. No motivation is ever as pressing as the need to say something on a subject that matters urgently to you. Your first task is to find an approach to the topic capable of moving you to care and to work and to write. If you can find such an approach, the process of writing — the reading, the thinking, even the reworking of your thoughts — will be carried along by the desire to know and not only by the need to complete the assignment.

## Pertinence

An essay should not be a trivial pursuit. It should matter to you and to its reader. As you shape your thesis statement, keep the *value* of your subject in mind. When selecting a point of view, allow yourself to think about its broader implications, even if there is no place to include all of these in the essay itself. You don't have to tell readers how relevant your topic is, but you should believe it, and you should be able to show that you do. Ensuring that your perspective is new and making your point of view matter to your reader are fundamental requirements.

## Proportion

The thesis statement indicates what size the essay will be in its finished form. A well-measured thesis statement is snug, not loose, in its fit. If it does not fit properly, the arguments that follow may sag. To ensure a good fit between thesis statement and essay, ask questions. Ask yourself if there is room in a 1500-word essay to discuss all the implications of unemployment in Canada. If not, then trim the thesis statement to fit: e.g., unemployment among students seeking part-time jobs in Canadian cities.

## Precision

As in a legal contract, the essay is the delivery of promises made in its thesis statement. And, as with all such contracts, the issues to be dealt with must be clarified at the outset. Make sure before you develop your thesis statement that you have made clear to your readers both what your essay will do *and* what it will *not* do. Feel free to announce (without apologies) in or near the thesis statement what the limits of your treatment of the subject are.

## Point

Not only should your thesis statement have a point to make, it must point in a particular direction. A useful addition to the thesis statement itself is the "route map." The route map informs readers of the highlights of the journey they are about to make. For instance, in a sociology essay comparing the changing attitudes toward women in advertisements from the 1940s to the 1990s, as reflected in two issues of the same magazine, you can briefly outline the steps in your discussion:

> *Three major changes can be noted in the presentation of female figures: women are shown less often in domestic situations; women are more often featured as authority figures; and women are more often shown in active, rather than passive, roles.*

Such a statement contains the direction of the entire essay in miniature and points toward the arguments to follow.

## Now that you have a thesis statement . . .

Use your thesis statement as the springboard for the outline. Keep it in mind as you develop your thought. With your thesis statement on paper, you are now ready to set the tone for the readers you have in mind.

## CHAPTER 1 EXERCISES

1. Develop a focus for the following topics, using some of the techniques listed above. Each is meant to be the subject of a 1500-word essay in the discipline suggested.

   a. child abuse (Sociology)
   b. the role of women in the church (Religious Studies)
   c. the relationship of sports to national unity (Physical Education)
   d. management styles (Business Administration)
   e. Native rights (History)
   f. female characters in Shakespeare's history plays (English)
   g. learning disabilities (Education)
   h. the right to die (Philosophy)
   i. globalization and national identity (Political Science)
   j. the effect of immigration on culture (Sociology)

2. Examine some of your past essays to see if the thesis statements you have written have narrowed the topic down sufficiently. Try rewriting them to give them more focus.

3. Develop a thesis statement for each of the following topics:

   a. attitudes toward money
   b. styles of parenthood
   c. entrance marks and higher education
   d. knowing when to quit
   e. approaches to learning
   f. keeping quiet
   g. your goals
   h. attitudes toward aging
   i. finding a job
   j. choosing courses

4. Evaluate these thesis statements:

   a. There are pros and cons that must be considered when one decides whether to go away to school.
   b. Shakespeare's comedies explore the supremacy of women over men.
   c. Arts funding in Canada is largely based on government grants.

# Setting Tone

> A great many people now reading and writing
> would be better employed keeping rabbits.
>
> *Edith Sitwell*

Tone is one of the most elusive features of a writing style, whether your own or someone else's. The tone of your essay writing, if it is to avoid clashing with the reader's expectations, should be neither too loud nor too soft. Harsh tones may antagonize your readers. Conversely, gentle tones may make your arguments seem too weak or too bland.

Tone in writing may be compared to tone of voice. It is the personality of an essay. What follows will show both which tones to avoid and which to emulate. When you read your paper aloud to check for errors at the revision stage, you will listen for potential problems. But even before you write, it is important to think about the impact of your ideas on the readers.

The tone you choose must fit the purposes of your essay. If the assignment is a formal research paper, the tone must be appropriately formal as well. If, on the other hand, you are writing an informal, more personal paper, your tone may be correspondingly more casual. The expectations of your readers define the tone for you.

In large part, setting tone is a process of audience analysis. In order to communicate with your audience effectively, your writing must show that it takes the reader's reactions seriously. Some of the preparation you go through to write an essay necessarily involves anticipation of how your audience is likely to react to your subject. When you have thought about the potential problems, you are ready to set the tone of your paper.

## ■ Tones to Avoid

### Avoid whispering

A tone that is too "soft" suggests that the writer is unsure of the words and the thoughts behind them. Words that are too tentative, too hesitant, are one sign of a whispering tone. Phrases like "it seems to be" or "perhaps" or "it could be that" are indications of the problem. Another signal is the overuse of qualifying phrases such as "however" and "to some extent." Although some qualifications are a good idea, too many may cause the reader to doubt your confidence in your own position.

## Avoid chatting

A chatty essay is most often the result of incomplete planning and outlining. If your paragraphs or your sentences seem to trail off or to lead to unexpected conclusions, if your ideas seem linked by random association, if your language seems too colloquial or offhand, and if you treat the reader as a chum rather than as an interested observer, you may be accused of chattiness. The cure for chattiness is care, revision, and a polite, though distanced, regard for the reader.

## Avoid emotiveness

An emotive tone is struck when a writer attempts to describe his or her feelings in a high-flown, exaggerated way. Often, what results sounds falsely sentimental or hackneyed. Such a tone is often found in introductions and conclusions, particularly when a writer tries to wax poetic about his or her opinions. Although opinions are warranted in an essay, it is nevertheless not necessary to praise Shakespeare as a great playwright at the end of a paper analyzing the structure of *Macbeth*, or to tell the reader of an essay on nuclear disarmament that the issue is a matter of life and death for the human race. Show your feelings by supporting your opinions; don't just declare them.

## Avoid declaiming

Treat your reader as an equal. Though you may well be playing the role of expert, your role is to reason with your reader and to assume his or her rationality. Any style that repeats points too often, or goes on too long, or explains more than the reader needs is declaiming. This tactic, in combination with a pretentious vocabulary, is disastrous. When you revise, check to see that your writing is transparent, that it does not need to be deciphered to be understood. Avoid words that intimidate the reader because of their length or their obscurity. Choose instead the word that will most clearly express your meaning. Check also to see that the essay is within the required word limit.

In a formal essay, it is also wise to limit the use of rhetorical questions, or to avoid them altogether. Your job is to tell the reader something, not to ask questions.

## Avoid shouting

Make sure that your essay does not inadvertently antagonize its readers. Even though it is your job to defend your viewpoint, you must not assume that your readers are opponents. This problem with tone is especially prevalent in essays that attempt to refute someone else's position. In these cases, the force should be in the logic of your argument, rather than in the tone of your writing.

## Use personal pronouns with discretion

Avoid directly addressing your reader in formal essays. "You" and "your" may alienate the readers if your assumptions about their knowledge or their attitudes are incorrect. It may even sound cheeky or overbearing. If you can, keep the readers on your side; if you know they disagree, keep them at a formal distance.

A research or formal expository essay also may demand that you avoid the use of "I" in writing. If you are forbidden the use of "I" by an instructor, respect that condition.

Do, however, try to avoid awkward impersonal constructions and self-conscious references. Never refer to yourself as "the writer" or "the author."

On the other hand, if "I" is acceptable, *use* it. Your relationship to your reader in a formal essay is meant to be a professional one, but that does not mean that personality has no place, simply that you must know its place, and respect the polite distance imposed between you and the reader.

### *Example*

    ✗ *It is the opinion of this writer that . . .* (too stuffy)
    ✗ *In my opinion . . .* (too weakly subjective)

    ✓ *This paper contends that . . .*
    ✓ *I will show that . . .*

## ■ Tones to Emulate

### Modulate your writing style

A modulated voice is controlled. Despite the moods of the writer, it shows restraint, politeness, and judgement. Your tones in private conversation may be more varied; in the essay, however (except in the freer personal essay), your tone should be cool, professional, unruffled, and firm.

### Imitate the best

Read newspaper editorials and news magazines, as well as your fellow students' essays. Textbooks and critical material may also serve as examples, though you must choose with discretion. And listen. The tone of classroom lectures is often a good indication of what is expected in a paper.

---

### CHAPTER 2 EXERCISE

Find an essay in a learned journal and analyze its tone. Do the same with an article in a popular magazine. Describe the tone of both pieces. How do the works differ in terms of audience and purpose? Compare them in terms of vocabulary, use of personal pronouns, use of specialized language, complexity of sentence structure, and assumptions about the reader's familiarity with and interest in the subject under discussion. How is the tone, whether formal or informal, created in each case?

# Choosing Words: Avoiding Jargon, Slang, and Stereotypes

> Words are all that we have.
>
> *Samuel Beckett*

Word choice is perhaps the most accurate index of the status of a writer. The words you choose depend in part on the role you mean to play in relation to the reader.

Not only is word choice important to tone, but it is also crucial to clarity. The words you use should be weighed carefully: you need to be fully conscious of all the nuances of meaning that they may conjure up. We often use words in a number of quite different ways; if we substitute one for another too blithely, we may find ourselves rather embarrassed. Take, for example, the simple adjective "dirty." If you were to look it up in a thesaurus, you would find a list of words, including, perhaps, "soiled," "unclean," "polluted," "filthy," "foul," "lewd," and "obscene." In this example, it is obviously not adequate to substitute "lewd" for "dirty" in the context of someone's dirty hands. Exact meaning is absolutely demanded if word choice is to be clear.

Good writing demands more than clarity, however. It demands attention to the delicate relationship it has with a reader. It must strive not to say more than it intends, or to create unpleasant, unsuitable, or ludicrous associations in the reader's mind. When you choose your words, stay aware not only of their denotations, but also of their connotations. It is now, for example, important to use language that is deliberately inclusive. While standard grammar used to sanction the use of "his" or of generic words like "men" to mean "humans," readers are these days more likely to take issue with such an exclusive approach to the sexes. Here is another area that demands close attention if you are to form a good relationship with your reader.

### Write to impress — not to intimidate

When you write an essay, you should address your reader as an equal; the information you impart and the viewpoint you defend are offered as reasonable choices for readers as clear-thinking as you are.

To impress a reader, you need to show what you know and to express a willingness to share it. If your words do not allow you to share your results, because they are either too technical or too vague or carelessly chosen, you will have alienated your readers. Remember that, in the formal essay, the emphasis is less upon you and the reader personally than it is upon the subject at hand: your relationship is entirely professional. But in the informal essay, your personality and that of your reader play more pronounced roles: you expect that the reader will enjoy your company.

### Make yourself comfortable in the language of your subject

Determining your status, and thus the proper diction for an essay, is sometimes a great challenge. After all, you may not feel much like the equal of the professor giving a course in which you feel shaky or ill prepared. Obviously, the more conversant you become with the terminology of a discipline, the easier it will be to feel like an equal and to write a stimulating learned discussion.

Just as important, however, is the confidence with which you can play the role of an equal. Think of your paper not as just another assignment, written by a student to an instructor, but as an opportunity to speak the language of the discipline to someone who understands it.

### Choose your words stylishly

The "rules" that govern diction cannot be listed here, simply because word choice depends upon context. A formal essay demands formal language, just as a formal occasion demands evening dress. Likewise, informal writing allows you more freedom in self-expression and a more casual approach.

## ■ Diction: Fit, Form, and Function

Choose language that satisfies the criteria of fit, form, and function for the assignment in question. What follows are some pointers on how to choose (and to revise) the language of your essays.

### Observing the dress code

Paying attention to the conventions of a dress code does not mean that you must wear a uniform inhibiting all expression of personality. It means, simply, that you must conform to certain standards — happily, in this case, quite flexible standards.

Keep these guidelines in mind:

1. Fit — Does your writing suit its purpose and audience?
2. Form — Does it conform to convention?
3. Function — Does your writing make your message clear?

If the idea of conforming for the sake of conforming disturbs you, remember what the consequences of not conforming may be: perhaps being misunderstood, ignored, or considered offensive. To avoid any of these perils in your use of language, and in your word choice particularly, keep these hints in mind.

## Avoid over-dressed language

### 1. Do not use too many technical or specialized terms or acronyms.

Too many terms may actually prevent your reader from seeing your underlying meaning. Technical subjects clearly demand some technical terminology, but while it is partly your task to demonstrate your ability to use terms with skill and ease, you must not use them to confuse your reader or to avoid the issues. Acronyms like DAT (for "digital audio tape") may be meaningful to you, but if you intend to use such shortened forms throughout your essay, you should identify them at the outset in order to avoid confusion. The best form is to use the term in its entirety first: "Digital audio tape (DAT) is available to consumers who wish to make high-quality recordings in their own homes."

### 2. Avoid neologisms used out of context.

Words, like everything else, have a history. A word like "lifestyle," of modern derivation, is inappropriate when used to describe the feudal way of life, for example.

### 3. Avoid the current tendency to make nouns out of verbs.

"Impact" is a noun and not a verb; something may therefore "have an impact on" something, but may not "impact on" something. A similar problem occurs with words ending in "ize" and "ization." Many are now acceptable, but some are questionable recent coinages, often unnecessary and vague. "Prioritize," for example, should be replaced with "establish priorities."

### 4. Avoid pretentious words and constructions.

Often these pretentious constructions appear as groups of nouns, attached in such a way that the reader cannot visualize the object described. The tendency to use such abstract and depersonalized language comes partly from our desire to appear sophisticated, but the effect is rather like wearing designer labels on the outside of our clothes. Such a high-sounding style may intimidate or amuse, but it does not really communicate.

### Example

✗ *Mimi found it difficult to orientate herself in the library.*

Replace "orientate" with "orient." When in doubt, check usage in a dictionary or a guide to usage.

✗ *Irregardless of her negative attitude, Gloria got the job.*

Replace "irregardless" with "regardless." "Irregardless" is non-standard usage.

### 5. Avoid "flashy" words.

Sometimes a student will fervently consult a thesaurus, seeking some clever ways of varying vocabulary. Although this is a commendable practice, never forget that no two words mean exactly the same thing or have precisely the same impact. When you find a synonym, check it in the dictionary to make sure that it means what you think it does. Make sure your words know their place.

A longer word is not necessarily a stronger word. A word selected simply "for show" may be as out of place as a diamond tiara worn with a soccer uniform. Context is the first consideration in these matters. Don't use a word just because it sounds elevated.

## Example

> ✗ At any time of year, upon entering this voluminous structure, one cannot help but notice the low roar of conversation as the voices of the library's patrons reverberate from one concrete wall to the other.

How can a library be "voluminous"? Replace this word with something more suitable — like "huge" or "imposing."

## Avoid sloppy language

### 1.  Avoid slang.

There are, admittedly, times when slang fits the mood. You may, for instance, wish to draw attention to the common language for a particular term, or report some dialogue. Beware of enclosing slang in quotation marks ("swell"); it may seem forced and unnatural. Unless you are sure that slang will add colour and character to your writing, avoid it. Careless slang is sloppy and perhaps more revealing than you wish.

Try to be conscious of your use of slang. It is easy to pick up words and phrases that seem to be in vogue and to use them unthinkingly. A word or phrase that comes too easily will not help you do any original thinking; the reader may just glide over the usage without reflection as well. Worse still, the reader may not know the particular usage you have in mind.

## Examples

> ✗ I avoid reading psychology books because I think the subject is flaky.
> ✗ Mathematics boggles the mind.
> ✗ I was really out to lunch on that last exam.

### 2.  Avoid colloquial constructions.

Colloquial constructions may include slang, but they also include language that is chatty, takes too much for granted, or is not completely clear. A carefully selected colloquial word or phrase may add unexpected life to a formal paper, but the overuse of language generally confined to speech may lead the reader to dismiss the value and importance of what you are saying.

Because you have no chance to reinforce your words with body language (a raised eyebrow, a smile, a frown), your reader will need the most precise, specific language you can possibly find. You need all the power and clarity of the words at your command.

*Example*

---

✗ *Voters were initially enthused with Jean Chrétien's plans to increase employment among Canadians.*

Replace "enthused with" with "enthusiastic about."

### 3. Avoid saying the obvious, especially in a hackneyed way.

What you have to say may not be entirely new, but your approach to the subject should be fresh, and your way of expressing yourself should give the reader a new angle of perception.

Avoid language deadened by overuse, whether it be jargon or cliché. Use language that enlightens, that sparks thought, that provokes discussion, that wakes up your reader. Saying the same old thing in the same old way may be the easy way out, but it will not have the same impact that a thoughtful or inventive use of words may have.

The cliché does, however, have its place. For instance, in the paragraph above, the phrase "the easy way out" is a cliché. In the midst of some fairly abstract prose, its presence can startle just because it is a different kind of language than what precedes it. Use clichés sparingly, and don't use them thoughtlessly. Otherwise they may have all the impact of a joke too often repeated.

*Example*

---

✗ *Those who are employed in the service industry often feel they are working for peanuts.*

Replace "working for peanuts" with fresher, more thoughtful phrasing, perhaps "they are not paid enough to eat properly."

### 4. Consult a dictionary to find the proper usage of a word.

When you look up a word in the dictionary, you will find information vital to its usage. Usually, one of the first things you will see in a listing is an abbreviation which denotes what part of speech the word is. For example, if you look up the word "impact," you will find it listed as a noun. If you are in doubt about what any of the abbreviations used in your dictionary mean, check them in the list of abbreviations, usually provided at the beginning of the dictionary. Also pay special attention to samples of idiomatic usage that may be given; such examples may offer you more help in how to use a word more accurately than an abstract knowledge of its meaning alone. Dictionaries give current information about how to use a word in standard English: they are reliable sources in determining whether a word's usage is archaic, dialect, colloquial, or slang.

### 5. Be especially careful to avoid bias in your language.

Unintended bias occurs when people are not scrupulously careful about their language. To avoid bias, you should be sure to use inclusive language. For example, in a letter you should use the salutation "Dear Sir or Madam" rather than "Dear Sir" if you are unsure of the recipient's identity, thus avoiding accusations of sexism. You should be cautious about assuming things; make sure that you respect the terms that individuals or groups use to identify themselves rather than assigning labels to them. This tactic usually assures that you will be using a specific term rather than a generalized, or even a stereotypical one. For instance, the word "Korean" is more specific than "Asian" and may be more accurate. Be wary of "pseudogeneric" words such as "mankind" or "chairman" that seem to be inclusive but are not. "Humankind" and "chair" are preferred in these cases. Make sure that the language you choose treats everyone equally. An expression like "the man and his wife" does not accord equal treatment: substitute either "the man and the woman" or "the husband and wife." Why, after all, should one of the individuals be identified only in relation to the other? Finally, it is always a good idea to use a term that puts people first. Do not say "the disabled," but "people with disabilities," or, if the characteristic is irrelevant, don't mention it at all.

## CHAPTER 3 EXERCISES

1. Make a list of common expressions we use to describe talking. The list might include such phrases as "chewing the fat." Try to analyze the origins and the functions of these expressions. Do the same thing with words and expressions used to describe eating.

2. Find clichés or overused expressions that you or the people you talk to are fond of. Analyze whether this language is effective in the contexts in which you find it.

3. Clichés often take the form of comparisons, such as he felt "fresh as a daisy" or it was "clear as mud." Make a list of three of these expressions, and then vary them by drawing new comparisons.

4. Read over essays you have written, and note any clichés, jargon, or bias you find. Rephrase the sentences, substituting fresh language.

5. A. Identify problems in the following sentences and suggest alternative wording. Turn to p. 200 to check your answers.

    1. I enjoy gambling, but I get annoyed when other people welsh on a bet.
    2. Martin asked Darlene to have dinner with him, but she refused because he wanted to go Dutch treat, and her payday wasn't until Friday.
    3. Mailmen are frequently bitten by unfriendly dogs.
    4. The girl at the desk was extremely polite to the customers.
    5. We were encouraged to avoid thinking about issues as if they were black or white.
    6. The retarded were put in a special class.
    7. Her mother is just about ready to go into an old people's home.
    8. A victim of polio, Allan sustained permanent damage to his muscles.
    9. Working women must deal with many complicated demands on their time.
    10. Unwed mothers are the main recipients of welfare.

    B. Identify problems in the following sentences and suggest alternative wording.

1. Elizabeth has long been a divorcée.
2. Edith Piaf was an accomplished songstress.
3. Stricken by a chronic ailment, arthritics suffer considerable pain upon arising.
4. Bettina is confined to a wheelchair.
5. Sandra Oh, the actress who appeared in *Oleanna*, is an Asian girl.
6. He refused to go to a lady doctor.
7. She wanted to learn everything there was to know about the history of mankind.
8. Sheila Copps delivered a feisty address to Parliament.
9. She was a working mother.
10. Many Canadian Indians still live on the reservation.

# PART TWO

# Designing the Essay

# Designing an Outline

> The discipline of the writer is to learn to be still
> and listen to what the subject has to tell him.
> *Rachel Carson*

O nce you have decided upon your topic, determined your thesis statement, and considered your audience and purpose, you need an outline.

Never attempt to write an essay without some kind of outline — whether it be a formal, detailed itinerary or a hastily jotted map showing your destination, your direction, and the stops you wish to make along the way.

When preparing an outline, remember that it is only a sketch of your paper. The final design of the essay may be quite different from what you originally intended. A sketch does not need to be perfect. The outline is meant to help you write the paper, not to restrict your line of thought. Keep the outline flexible so that you can tinker with it as you go along. It is simply a tentative blueprint, a description of the contents of your paper, rather than a prescription of its requirements.

## ■ Make a Table of Contents

Think of the outline as your own flexible table of contents. It is, after all, your note to yourself, your reminder of what details you wish to include and what arguments you want to make. Like a table of contents, the outline labels what the reader may expect to find contained in the work itself.

Take a look at the table of contents of this book to see what information can be gleaned from it. Not only does it tell you *what* is included in the book, it tells you what the major and minor divisions of the work are. For instance, you will find the chapter entitled "Devising a Thesis" under the part heading "Developing the Essay."

In other words, the table of contents gives the reader a sense of the book's dimensions. You see, for example, that the book you are holding in your hand has seven major parts, each of which is divided into a number of chapters. Thus, it gives you a sense not only of the work's overall shape, but also of the size of each component, and, at the same time, of the orderly arrangement of its position within the work. What follows is not a set of rules for composing outlines, but a series of suggestions about what they may contain.

To make your outline as useful and as organized as a table of contents, keep the following steps in mind:

## ■ Sort Through Your Ideas

### 1. Make sure you have established your pivotal points: the thesis statement and purpose.

Use your thesis statement (subject to revision) and your selected purpose as the launching points for your outline. From them will emanate all the ideas, arguments, facts, and figures you have gathered.

### 2. Gather your notes.

With your tentative thesis statement on paper in front of you, gather your tentative remarks, your research, and your questions about the topic. One good way to take notes is to list separate ideas on index cards (remembering to include sources, if any). This way, you can shuffle or discard material easily.

Keeping your purpose in mind, organize the material you have selected, discarding any information not strictly related to it. If you are discussing kinds of stage props, for instance, don't include material on their development in the history of the theatre.

### 3. Classify your material.

Decide how many steps your argument contains. Then classify your notes accordingly. If, for example, you mean to consider three reasons that Japanese businesses outrank their Canadian counterparts, decide in which of the three discussions to include a statistic about productivity growth.

### 4. Order your material in a logical way.

This process demands that you decide at what point a particular argument should be mentioned. Here you must decide what your opening argument, your follow-up, and your last word should be. Keep in mind the tried-and-true notion that a strong point is best placed at the beginning or ending of an essay. Keep in mind, too, that some of your organizational decisions are dependent upon the pattern of argument you selected at the outset. If you know, for instance, that your reader will need to understand your definition of a crown corporation to get the most out of your essay, put it where it will be most accessible. Or, if you are explaining a process, make sure the reader is able to follow it step by step.

### 5. Rank your points according to their importance.

Sorting your ideas according to rank means deciding whether an item has a major role or merely a minor one to play. The ranking itself will give you an excellent idea of what you have to say and of how developed your thought is. Where you have much to add or to explain, the idea is vital and may serve as a significant part of your argument; where your idea is almost all you have to say on the subject, you may relegate the point to a minor status.

In order to rank your ideas, assign them numbers or letters, beginning perhaps with capital Roman numerals for major sections, moving to capital letters for important supporting sections, through to Arabic numbers for less important support material, to small letters for the minor details. The points you are making are primary in rank; the support you gather for them is secondary.

### *Example*

    *I.  Japan outranks Canada in productivity for two reasons.*
        *A.  Japanese companies are especially concerned with employee relations. (REASON #1)*
           *1.  Employees are often hired for life, not for limited periods, as often is done in Canada.*
           *2.  Employees are given greater benefits and security than in Canadian companies.*
              *a.  They are encouraged to participate in decisions more often than is the case in Canada.*
              *b.  Their jobs are usually more stable than ours, though lower wages are sometimes the result.*
              *c.  Japanese workers are treated like family members, rather than as employees.*
        *B.  Japanese companies place special emphasis on technological advancements. (REASON #2)*
           *1.  Technological advancement has permitted more efficient quality control.*
              *a.  "Computerized" and "robotized" assembly lines have decreased the margin of error.*

The form of notation does not matter particularly, but it should permit you to see *at a glance* the relative scope of the point you are making. A carefully ranked outline will show you the ideas within ideas.

## 6. Invent a title.

Although you still have not arrived at a finished product, the argument you make in your essay should be clear enough to you that a title should pose no problem. Just bear in mind that a title should give the reader specific information about the subject you are writing about. Don't entitle your paper "Margaret Atwood"; instead, call it "The Function of Autobiographical Form in Atwood's *Cat's Eye*." Do not underline your title; reserve underlining for the titles of published works. A title should be catchy and not too lengthy, but don't sacrifice clarity for flourish.

## ■ Tailor the Outline

As you outline, you may well notice some rags and tatters among your papers, bits of research material that seemed valuable at the time you took the notes, though they now seem unrelated to the development of your thought. If you cannot use these scraps in the final fabric of your argument, do not hesitate to toss them out. Remember that one of the main functions of the outline is to show you how well the material you have gathered actually fits the viewpoint you have chosen. Each point of the outline ought to represent an area that you can fill with developed thoughts, facts, and evidence. If you find that all you have to say on a particular point can be fleshed out in one sentence, then you must find a way to incorporate that small point into another place in your argument, or perhaps you may have to eliminate it altogether. What isn't useful or appropriate for your thesis statement should be left behind.

The outline below shows a short persuasive essay developed by examples, definition, classification, and even comparison/contrast. Basically, the essay consists of three arguments to defend the thesis, plus supporting arguments. These patterns of argument will be discussed in the next chapter.

Note that each section has a small thesis statement (or topic sentence) of its own. These are best written as sentences in the outline to ensure clarity. Note also that the subdivisions allow you to see at a glance what items have the most support (and conversely, what might be in need of greater support or development).

### *A sample student outline*

TOPIC: Headaches
PATTERN OF ARGUMENT: Classification

I. INTRODUCTION: Everyone suffers a headache at one time or another, though the pain can vary in degree. Some headaches respond to aspirin; others are excruciating, perhaps chronic or debilitating.
THESIS STATEMENT: In order to treat a headache properly, one must be able to diagnose it correctly.
PREVIEW: There are four types of headache: the tension headache, the cluster headache, the sinus headache, and the migraine.

II. BODY
  A. A tension headache
    a. Cause: muscle contraction
    b. Symptoms: dull, steady ache; tightness around the scalp or neck
    c. Triggers: stress, anxiety, repressed emotion
    d. Treatment: aspirin
  B. A cluster headache
    a. Cause: unknown
    b. Symptoms: burning, piercing pain, often behind one eye; occurs periodically for days, weeks, or months; less than an hour in duration
    c. Triggers: smoking, alcohol consumption, histamines, or nitroglycerine
    d. Treatment: medication, such as ergotamines, inhaled or held under the tongue
  C. A sinus headache
    a. Cause: any disturbances blocking the passage of fluid from the sinuses
    b. Symptoms: gnawing pain, rise in temperature
    c. Triggers: same as cause
    d. Treatment: nasal decongestants and antibiotics
  D. A migraine
    a. Cause: not known

b. Symptoms: nausea, dizziness, cold hands, tremor, sensitivity to light and sound; sometimes a day or longer in duration

c. Triggers: irregular eating and sleeping; ingestion of cheese, chocolate, red wine, or caffeine

d. Treatment: no cure, but some medications prevent or abort headaches; lifestyle changes are recommended

**III.** CONCLUSION: Relief from headaches is possible for most people if they learn to seek the safest and most effective treatment available.

## CHAPTER 4 EXERCISES

1. Develop outlines, complete with thesis statements, for the following topics:

   a. student newspapers
   b. the homeless
   c. the importance of rituals
   d. the cost of living well
   e. time management
   f. getting along with people
   g. movie censorship
   h. manners

2. Reread an essay you have written for a course in the past and sketch an outline of its structure. Is each section clearly delineated? Is adequate support given for each point that you raise? Is the movement of the paper logical and easy to follow? Would you do anything differently in light of the outline you have produced?

3. Read an essay you find in a journal related to your field of study. Make an outline of it, complete with thesis statement, arguments, and support.

4. Find a set of instructions, perhaps something as simple as a recipe. Analyze how the information is put together in order to make the process clear to the reader. Write an outline and a set of instructions of your own that describe a simple task.

# Choosing a Pattern of Argument

I think you can't learn to write, and people who spend money on writing courses would do much better to send the money to me, and I'll introduce them to an editor.

*Fran Lebowitz*

After you have established your thesis statement and made your outline, you need to choose the pattern or patterns of argument that will do it justice. Usually an essay will demand several patterns in support of its thesis, as the sample outline in the preceding chapter demonstrates. In order to support your thesis with a similar variety of arguments, you must look for methods by which to direct your thought. The following tactics may serve as structural guidelines or blueprints for your thought:

Definition/Description
Example
Classification
Comparison/Contrast
Cause/Effect
Narration

These patterns cannot be entirely separated from each other. Usually, a writer will use several patterns to develop one essay. Refer, for example, to the outline in the preceding chapter. It uses many different kinds of argument, including definition, classification, comparison/contrast, and example.

A paragraph that defines "dreams," for example, may contrast a simple dictionary definition with a more elaborate definition offered by a psychologist. Examples of dreams may be given to show something about their essential nature, perhaps demonstrating the creativity of the unconscious mind.

The patterns listed below should offer you some inspiration when you get stuck in the process of outlining your thought. Refer to this section when you need help in the amplification of an argument.

# ■ Definition/Description

Definition suggests the use of a dictionary to define a term explicitly. This tactic ensures that there is a general consensus between writer and readers as to the term's meaning in the context of the essay.

Although dictionary definitions are important, don't rely too heavily on them. Belabouring a definition already familiar to your readers may alienate them: it may sound condescending. Furthermore, a critical reader will be concerned more with what you *make* of a definition than with its content per se. If you do cite a dictionary definition, make sure that you use it to make a point.

What comprises a useful definition? First, it must supply the reader with characteristics that describe something. Occasionally, it may describe by way of comparison/contrast, by showing what the thing is not. And, it may give some enlightening history of the term, showing how it came to have the meaning it has. It may then show what something does, in order to describe more concretely what it is. Lastly, it may give an example, meant to epitomize the nature of the thing described.

## *Example*

What, exactly, is a dream? Webster's *says nothing more than that it is a "hallucination in sleep."[1] This rather bland attempt at definition masks the essential problem. The truth is that we do not really know what dreams are, though there has always been a great deal of speculation about their nature. Some modern psychologists, such as Carl Jung, maintain that dreams are unconscious subjective recreations of reality: "the dream is the theater where the dreamer is at once scene, actor, prompter, stage manager, author, audience, and critic."[2] But, even among modern psychologists, there is still considerable disagreement about the source of dreams.*

This definition introduces the subject and provides two possible definitions of what dreams are.

# ■ Example

Because readers usually find it easier to understand what they can picture, examples are often the best means of amplifying an argument. Whether you use an extended example, meant to illustrate your general point in a series of specific ways, or whether you use a variety of small examples to achieve the same end, examples lend support to your argument.

## *Example*

One of the most famous recorded dreams is Kekulé's account of his discovery of the nature of benzene. In 1865, Kekulé, a chemist, fell asleep and dreamt of a snake with its tail in its mouth.[3] His intuition about the structure of benzene — that its molecules were not open structures but rings — was one of the cornerstones of modern scientific thinking. This episode illustrates that some dreams have a creative component capable of communicating, in a flash, something that the conscious mind has been seeking in vain. Some dreams apparently can bring about a breakthrough in understanding.

This example supports the idea that dreams are sometimes creative.

# ■ Classification

In order to explain something more precisely, a writer often has recourse to methods of classification, by which he or she can make necessary distinctions within a subject area. Classifying different parts of a subject involves making decisions about what belongs where. A large subject may be divided into smaller or more manageable sections to make important distinctions clear. In order for classification to work convincingly, the reader must be assured that the categories are tidy, include everything essential, and do not substantially overlap.

## *Example*

> Although dreams have been a subject of much study throughout history, there is still no consensus about what dreams mean. Some philosophers, like Bertrand Russell, contend that dreams cannot be differentiated from reality, that, in fact, we do not know which is real, the waking state or the dreaming state.[4] Others maintain, even in certain modern cultures, that dreams have divinatory qualities that tell us something about what might happen. Modern psychologists argue that dreams are proof of unconscious activity in the mind, and their studies of dreams seek to understand the springs of behaviour.

This classification lists some of the different interpretations of what dreams mean.

# ■ Process

It is often necessary in the course of an essay to explain how to do something or how something works. When describing a process, think of yourself as a teacher. It is part of your job to supply your readers with all the information they require to understand, without confusion, a given process. At the same time, you must be careful to assess their level of understanding accurately, if you are to avoid writing that is boring or condescending. It is also part of your job to present the material in a logical, step-by-step manner, so that the reader is spared needless cross-referencing and rereading. Check your description of the process to see if its steps can be easily followed.

## *Example*

> The Freudian view of the process of dreaming, recorded in The Interpretation of Dreams in 1899, suggests that dreams are stimulated by bodily reactions, experiences during daylight hours, and infantile memories. When people dream, according to Freud, they give way to primitive impulses, to repressed wishes, often displaced or represented in symbolic terms. When they awaken, dreamers revise their dreams by rationalizing and elaborating upon their reports of them. To understand these subconscious processes, Freud suggested that the content of dreams be analyzed through free association that would allow the dreamer to become aware of the hidden meanings and symbols of the dream.[5]

This paragraph outlines the steps in Freud's interpretation of the process of dreaming.

## ■ Comparison/Contrast

Comparisons are an essential part of expository writing. No pattern of argument is more common on examination questions, for instance, than comparison/contrast.

A comparison includes both similarities and differences. When you contrast, however, you focus exclusively on the differences between things.

When comparing, keep the overall structure in mind. You may present first one thing and then the other, or you may present the two things in combination. Alternating between the two is best if the material to be covered is complex or lengthy.

### *Example*

> From earliest times, there has been sharp disagreement about the sources of dreams. One school of thought sees dreams as a natural phenomenon; the other sees them as something supernatural. Even the basic division between Freud and Jung on the nature of dreams can be seen this way. Freud holds that dreams are explainable in terms of what he calls "day residue" and of external stimuli;[6] that is, they are borrowed from the images of daily life accompanied by bodily disturbances. Together these elements produce a dream that reveals much about the dreamer's repressed desires and feelings. Jung's account of the source of dreams is more spiritual and less a part of natural human functions. He argues that a "dream is the small hidden door in the deepest and most intimate sanctum of the soul"[7] and his studies of individuals' dreams attempt to relate the dreamer to the larger patterns of human consciousness throughout history.

This paragraph illustrates the main differences between Jung and Freud on the subject of dreams.

## ■ Cause and Effect

This pattern traces the relationship between the cause of an event or a condition and its results. When seeking to develop an argument by tracing causes and their effects, keep in mind two potential dangers. First, beware of trusting the idea of causality too much. Simply because one thing follows another chronologically does not mean that the second event was caused by the first.

Second, do not limit effects to one cause alone. Usually more than one determinant brings about an event or a trend. Don't wear blinkers in your zeal to establish connections.

### *Example*

> Recent studies show that there is a physiological correlation between sleep patterns and the frequency of dreams. In the 1950s, researchers found a link between bursts of rapid eye movement (sometimes called REM sleep), increased electrical activity in the brain, and frequency of reported dreams. If a dreamer is awakened during a period of REM sleep, there is a much greater chance that he or she will report and remember a dream. These studies show that dreams usually, though not always, occur in conjunction with certain patterns of activity in the dreamer's brain.[8]

This paragraph points out a relationship between sleep patterns and dreams. It also illustrates one of the problems in establishing an argument; note that while the author of the paragraph does mention a correlation between two things, there is no claim of a definite cause-and-effect relation between them. Often, there can be no positive declaration of cause and effect. Be cautious in your claims.

# ■ Narration

Telling a story, like telling a good joke, is hard to do. You narrate, or tell a story, in a piece of expository writing in order to bring your argument to life.

To be effective, the narrative you use in an essay should contain carefully selected, telling details — enough to be vivid, not so many that it is boring. The narrative must be well timed: it should draw your reader into the writing or graphically illustrate a point you are making. It should hold the reader's attention: do not expand the story endlessly with "and then . . . and then . . . and then."

Use narration sparingly in essay writing. Most commonly, you will find it used to relate case studies, brief anecdotes, and extended examples.

## *Example*

> The Bible contains many stories of dreams used as prophecies. Perhaps the most famous is the story of the dreams of the Pharoah of Egypt. He dreamed of seven fat cattle, followed by seven lean cattle, which devoured the first. Then he dreamed of seven good stalks of corn, which were destroyed by seven lean stalks of corn. These dreams Joseph interpreted as prophecies about the fate of Egypt. First, it would experience seven years of plenty, then seven years of famine. In response to Joseph's interpretation, the Pharoah stored enough food from the seven good years to protect the country from starvation during the famine that followed.[9] Such treatments of dreams as prophecy are part of many religions and illustrate the captivating power of the dream on the human imagination.

This paragraph retells a familiar biblical story to make a point about the imaginative appeal of dreams.

The superscript numerals used throughout the sample paragraphs indicate places where a writer would have to acknowledge sources. In this case, traditional note numbers have been used. For more information on the subject of citation of sources, see Chapters 13 and 14.

# ■ Tips on Choosing the Right Pattern

Your choice of pattern may depend to some extent on your subject. In English, for example, one of the most common patterns is *Comparison/Contrast*. In Political Science and Sociology, you may find yourself most often choosing *Definition* or *Classification*. History makes most use of the *Cause/Effect* pattern. The most common pattern in all writing is *Example*. Choose your pattern wisely; keep its relevance to the overall thesis statement always in mind.

---

**CHAPTER 5 EXERCISES**

1. Develop the following thesis statements by using at least two appropriate patterns of argument:

a. The state of the environment demands our immediate attention.
b. The requirements for college and university admission need to be reassessed.
c. Nationalism needs to be replaced by global consciousness.
d. The mass media interfere with individual privacy.
e. Let the buyer beware!

2. Develop a thesis statement for one of the following topics:

a. Canada's relation to America
b. the advantages or disadvantages of technology

For the topic chosen, develop a short introductory paragraph ending with the thesis statement. Go through the patterns of argument listed, and decide which methods would be most appropriate for developing your thesis statement. Then, outline the essay.

3. Analyze the patterns of argument in a paper you have written in the past. What are your most common patterns? What patterns could be used more effectively?

4. Analyze the patterns of argument you find in an article selected from a journal or popular magazine. List any techniques you find that you could emulate in your own work.

5. Write a set of instructions for how to make something. The instructions should guide the reader clearly through the process involved to create the final product. Use the basic structure of a recipe as a guideline for your set of instructions, remembering to tell the reader what materials are needed and what methods are to be followed in a logical, step-by-step order.

6. Listen carefully to a speech delivered by a politician or a media celebrity, or study the text of a speech (sometimes these are available on-line). Take note of the techniques used to make an argument clear to an audience.

7. Write two definitions of a term you use in one of the disciplines you are studying. Design the first definition so it explains the term to a group of your peers; next, rewrite the definition so it is suitable for a grade one class. What techniques did you use to accomplish the second task?

8. Write an essay that compares two people you know. Obviously, you need to decide what the point of the comparison is first. For example, you might compare Margaret and David in order to show that one is a more loyal friend than the other, or to show that one of your friends is a more motivated student than another. Make sure that the comparison is not simply perfunctory; you are comparing the two people to explain something to the reader.

# PART THREE

# Drafting the Essay

# Shaping the Essay

> The wastepaper basket is the writer's best friend.
> *Isaac Bashevis Singer*

As you develop your outline from its bare structure to its fully dressed form, remember that the shape of the essay is in your hands. Though there are guidelines you can follow, the essay is not a form to be filled in. You create the form itself, by selecting what is included and what is left out.

## ■ The First Draft

To make the first draft of your essay easier to write, keep the following advice in mind:

### Write while you think, not after

To move from outline to essay, you need to develop your thought. This development does not involve long delays and cautious planning. Writing is not the expression of thought; it is thought itself. To avoid getting tangled up in a web of confusion, or worse, procrastination, write as you think, rather than after you have thought. Putting pen to paper, even in an unpolished way, will help you overcome the terror of the blank page and will enable you to examine your thoughts more objectively later on.

### Worry as you write

This may sound like odd advice in a book meant to help you compose an essay, but the worrying stage, uncomfortable though it may be, is usually productive. Worrying is thinking. Keep the essay in the back of your mind as you do other things; carry a small notebook and make a record of passing ideas.

### Plan to rewrite

Don't demand perfection of your prose the first time out. Writing demands rewriting, not only to correct, but to beautify as well. The need for revision does not mean that your first draft is a failure. Writers revise not only to correct errors, but also to find the smoothest, the most succinct, the most elegant way to say something. Writing without revision is like getting dressed without looking in a mirror.

## Allow yourself freedom to experiment

Say something. The essay is your chance to say what you want to say (within the limits of decorum!) the way you want to say it. All that is demanded in an essay assignment is that you think independently (and perhaps with a little help from source material) and write in your own words (perhaps with the occasional quoted expert). Don't allow the fear of criticism to paralyze you at the outset. In your first draft especially, write to suit yourself.

## Allow yourself space to write and to make mistakes

Double or triple space. Leave wide margins. Leave one side of the page blank. Use pencil if you like. Or use coloured markers so you can see immediately what is being added or deleted.

Cut and paste, literally (or with the aid of a word processor), in order to give yourself the chance to see the complete sequence of ideas.

## Develop your own methods of quick notation

As you write, include references immediately after their occurrence in the text. Generally, use the author's last name and a page number in parentheses just after the quotation or the reference in your paper. If you use the documentation suggested by the MLA or APA (see p. 125 of this volume), this notation may be all you need. If not, your notes can be amended later.

## If you are using a word processor

If you are lucky enough to be able to compose your essay on a word processor, take advantage of any of its special features that will enable you to write more quickly and efficiently. Here are some guidelines:

1. Experiment. Use the speed of the word processor to allow yourself a look at various possibilities in wording and in structure.
2. Write more critically than when you write on paper. Take advantage of the freedom from drudgery offered by the processor to move paragraphs and to revise wording.
3. Learn to proofread from the screen. Better still, double-check your proofreading. Check the screen first and then make a hard copy and check it.
4. Don't expect the machine to do everything for you. Even though the mechanical aspects of the essay should be simpler on a word processor, don't fool yourself that careful writing or rigorous revision can be eliminated.
5. Use the time you save by writing on a word processor to think your topic through more carefully, to do more intensive research, and to ferret out every small error.
6. Don't approach your paper as if it must be done in a linear fashion. Take advantage of the computer's ability to work on any section of your essay that you feel ready to tackle. If the introduction is giving you problems, skip over it for a while. Move on instead to some part of the paper over which you have more control. The writing process is recursive, rather

than linear; if technology permits, you can make your composition mirror the creative process.

7. Simplify your thinking about the revision process. When you come to revise your paper, there are only four operations available to you: you can add, delete, move, or change materials. The computer makes all these aspects of revision much easier than they are with pen and paper.

8. Since it is unusual for a writer to produce his or her best work in one single draft, you would be wise to save several drafts of your paper, shifting back and forth between them as you decide how best to express your ideas.

9. Take advantage of features that are often part of word processing software packages, such as the spell checker and the thesaurus. These functions are intended to help you overcome your own inadequacies as a writer and to speed up the entire process.

10. Let the speed that a word processor gives afford you the time to revise more carefully and rethink more deeply.

## ■ Assembling Evidence

### Remember the purpose of your research

Your research is intended to help you find support for the claims you make in your paper. Because an essay presents an argument, you want to confine your search to those things that will help you defend yourself: your evidence will explain why you think what you think and why your reader should be inclined to do so as well. Because the research is not meant to give you information on everything about the subject in question, and because what you are writing is an essay, not a report, you must keep this purpose firmly in mind.

### Determine what counts as evidence

In any kind of essay, there are really only four kinds of support that you could gather from your research materials: examples, statistics, authorities, and reasons. Seldom would you use all four kinds of evidence in any one short paper. When you assemble your research material, working outline in hand, you want to be able to isolate relevant parts of others' work to strengthen your own. Keep your priorities straight. What is important here is that you select research material relevant to your particular focus on the subject. Examples and reasons are more likely than the others to be drawn from your experience and from your own thinking, though this is not always the case; they are the commonest and closest to home, and may be either real or hypothetical. Often examples are the best way to make an abstract point concrete. Reasons, by contrast, represent your thoughts and questions about key terms and your critical evaluations of the arguments of others. Statistics and the citing of authorities are both useful methods of garnering support for your position. In both of these cases, however, you must be careful that you use the material in question and don't make the mistake of assuming that it speaks for itself; otherwise, your meaning will be obscured, and you will lose control over the paper itself. When you cite someone else's words, you must show the reader what you intended him or her to see in the passage; the meaning is not self-evident. Similarly, the meaning of a statistic must be related to your overall position in the paper; it is your responsibility to draw conclusions about what these findings mean for your claims.

## Make outlines of relevant arguments in the research

Strengthening your own case is often easier if you have made brief outlines or paraphrases of the arguments you encountered as you went along. It is often a wise idea to summarize your findings from a particular chapter or journal article in your own words, so that you can make the transition from notes to essay more smoothly. A summary of a journal article might consist of one page that outlined its thesis, its main points, an assessment of its support, and some general comments of your own in response to it. This method will record your engagement with your research materials better than any mere transcription of quoted materials might do.

## Take the opposition into account

The best approach to take with materials that argue against your position is to approach them head on, assuming, of course, that you have decided your position is reasonable and defensible. Once you make up your mind to argue on a particular side of a question, your best line of defence is to read opposing views carefully and use materials from them to show flaws in their thinking and your own counter-arguments. If you take this advice, your argument will be more complete and more encompassing in its perspective.

## Avoid "tunnel vision"

The success of your essay depends not only on your ability to make your case, but also on the maturity of your critical approach — your fairness, objectivity, and sensitivity to flaws in methodology (yours and others'). Don't let emotions prevent you from assessing the evidence. You may, for example, feel strongly that Canada should provide aid to developing countries, yet when writing an essay on the subject of development aid, you will have to assess the claims that such aid leads to economic dependency. Objectivity is essential.

## Interpret your findings

You cannot expect the citation of a statistic or the inclusion of a quotation to make your point. You must *interpret* the meaning of such evidence. A survey that indicates that 75 percent of the student population approves of aid to developing countries does not speak for itself. In order to interpret such findings, you need to know how many people were actually surveyed, whether or not the survey involved a fair random sampling, and whether the questions that made up the survey were clear and unbiased in their wording. Only when you have taken these factors into account can you use the figure to claim, for example, that the student population is, to a large extent, willing to support developing countries.

### Avoid "blind spots"

An essay demands that you take a position with regard to the evidence you uncover. That position must, however, be based on an objective and unbiased reading of the facts. To ensure that you do not wilfully (or otherwise) misread your evidence, try to formulate both the case for and the case against your position. Include in your essay not only a defence of your thesis, but also arguments that have led you to reject contrary interpretations. For example, if you are arguing that aid to developing countries is a humanitarian obligation, you must consider the charge that the resulting private foreign investment is exploitative. You may find that you must concede some points. Such qualification makes your argument all the more objective in its evaluation of the data.

### Aim at a better, not an ultimate, theory

When you use evidence to defend your thesis, be realistic in your goals. Your research and your thought together have led you to understand the data in a certain way. Your task is to show that your reading of the material exhibits common sense and attention to recent data. Your theory about the meaning of the evidence should help to explain something. You may find, for instance, that economic dependency only partly explains the continuing problems in developing countries and that internal, national factors play a part as well. Your theory won't be perfect — just the most reliable interpretation of the facts you have found.

## ■ The Conventional Shape of the Essay

In order to control your material, you must strive to achieve unity within your essay. An essay's unity is the wholeness of the vision, the focus that holds the disparate parts together. Without such wholeness, your essay will seem incomplete or rambling.

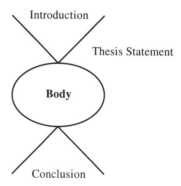

To do justice to your assembled arguments and support, the shape of your essay should meet certain of its readers' expectations. To make a good first impression on the reader, your essay should include these basic elements:

1. an *introduction*, moving from general topic to specific thesis, perhaps including a preview of its content;
2. a *body*, developing in turn each of the main points used to support your thesis statement;
3. a *conclusion*, reinforcing and/or summarizing what has been the focus of the essay and suggesting further implications.

Observing these conventional forms will ensure that your essay is clear, pointed, and emphatic from beginning to end.

A good essay possesses a sharp, comprehensive introduction and conclusion, with an expansive body that develops and supports the thesis.

## ■ Maintaining Unity in the Essay

An essay is a unit: a discussion centred on one basic point. Remember that your essay should focus on your thesis statement. An essay meant to grapple with the causes of the War of 1812 should not discuss its aftermath, just as an essay treating the issue of free will in *Paradise Lost* should find no place for a discussion of epic conventions.

To keep your essay unified:

1. Keep your purpose and basic pattern of argument firmly in mind.
2. Avoid digressions, however interesting, if they cannot be connected to the thesis statement.
3. Avoid padding for the sake of word length. Instead, develop your ideas by referring to Chapter 5, on patterns of argument, and relating them to your proposed thesis statement.
4. Redesign your thesis statement (within the limits of the assignment, of course), if you find your initial focus unappealing or too limited in scope.

Above all, remember the principle of unity:

**Everything in an essay should relate directly to the main focus of the paper.**

### CHAPTER 6 EXERCISES

1. Develop a line of argument in an outline for each of the following topics:
   a. Dangerous offenders should be executed.
   b. Computer courses should be mandatory.
   c. Fraternities and sororities should be disbanded.
   d. Student grant systems should be improved.
   e. Tobacco should be declared an illegal substance.
   f. School attendance should not be compulsory for children.

2. Read over an essay you wrote recently and note every time you digressed from the main focus of the essay and every time you added "padding."

# Making an Introduction

*0*

> The last thing we decide in writing a book is what
> to put first.
>
> *Blaise Pascal*

Think of your essay, for a moment, as if it were a person. Since an essay will establish some kind of relationship with its readers, the analogy is not altogether far-fetched. Here is some advice on how to proceed after you say "hello."

## ◼ Strike Up a Conversation

Obviously, writing a formal essay is more complicated than starting a conversation. But the analogy should provide you with a place to start. How should you begin a conversation? One way is to startle your listener by presenting an exciting piece of information, as a preview of coming attractions. Or, as a recommendation of the value of the work you have done, you can report the words of a well-known, respected authority in relation to your topic. Another method is to pick a fight, by stating the claims, or defining the terms, of the accepted position and then challenging them. Remember that your first task is to convince your audience to pay heed to what you are saying. What all of these tactics have in common is their ability to provoke a response.

Human judgement being the superficial, lazy thing it sometimes is (and professors are by no means exempt), an essay must overcome certain prejudices about its nature. In order to present itself proudly to an instructor, an essay must show immediate signs that it will not be boring, vague, pretentious, or long-winded.

## ◼ Write with Control

Perhaps the most common pitfall among essay writers in establishing the basis of their arguments is long-windedness. Remember that an introduction should be no longer than about one-fifth of the entire essay's length (the best introductions are short and comprehensive — don't go on). If you find that your introduction demands more space than that, you have not narrowed your topic down to a manageable size, or you should be writing a book instead! Never promise in the introduction more than you can deliver in the paper. The first few lines are the best place to limit the scope of your discussion and state the qualifications of your theories. Maintain control of your material, and have some consideration (if not some pity) for your poor beleaguered reader.

## ■ Write with Conviction

To avoid accusations of boredom, make sure that the introduction shows *how* what you have written matters — to you and to anyone concerned with the subject. Convincing readers that a topic is important is not simply a matter of telling them so; you have to show them, by the tone of your writing, that you are deeply engaged with the topic. Write with conviction, with the feeling that what you are saying will make a difference. Don't negate its value by suggesting that the essay's position is only your opinion. Approach the essay as if it were one side of a lively conversation. Because there is some distance between writer and reader, this interchange is not as immediate as that of conversation, but remember that there is a reader "at the other end of the line." Imagine your reader's responses as you introduce your material, just as you imagine your friend's face as she answers the telephone.

## ■ Be Conversant with Your Subject

Your introduction is meant to foster an existing knowledge and interest on the part of the reader. Don't tell the reader what he or she already knows. In the case of a literary essay, for example, there is no need to provide a plot summary. Any reader of such an essay should have that material well in hand. In other disciplines, this advice means avoiding the mere recital of material discussed in class, or the careful delineation of a definition that is neither contentious nor germane to what will follow. Write to communicate.

To avoid sounding pretentious, you must use your own voice and your sense of what is appropriate to the occasion. In the introduction, you must lead the reader into your way of thinking. The introduction must make both you and your reader comfortable. To get comfortable with a topic that, three weeks ago, may have been completely unfamiliar to you is part of the task of essay writing. Only when you can *talk* knowledgeably about the subject of your paper are you ready to write about it.

## ■ Communicate with Your Reader

If carefully designed, your introduction should tell the reader some essential things about you and your work: that you sincerely wish to communicate; that you are conversant with your subject and have convictions about it; that you are confident, in control, and considerate of your reader. All these nouns beginning with "con" or "com" suggest the necessity of forming a relationship *with* someone or something. An introduction with these attributes demands attention and commands respect.

# ■ Ice-Breaking: Tactics for Opening the Essay

If you are at a loss for words when writing your introduction, try one of the strategies in the following list. Suppose, for example, that your essay topic is "Man-made health hazards in the environment."

## 1. Take the straight and narrow path.

State your thesis bluntly and without preamble. Follow it with a brief statement of the steps in your argument.

*Example*

> *It is our fundamental human right to live in a healthy environment. For this to happen, we must protect the environment from man-made health hazards.*

## 2. Try shock treatment.

Give your reader a striking, perhaps shocking example, statistic, or statement to get him or her interested in reading further.

*Example*

> *One-year-old Diane Fowler woke up in the middle of the night in the midst of a convulsion. Her temperature was dangerously high. She was rushed to the Hospital for Sick Children in Toronto, where she was diagnosed as suffering from lead poisoning. Soon after, five more members of Diane's family were diagnosed as having lead poisoning. Within two years, a large group of citizens, all living near the Toronto-based lead plant, were found to have elevated levels of lead in their blood.*

## 3. Engage your reader.

Remind the reader that the subject under discussion matters to him or her by showing its general importance, before you settle down to your specific line of argument.

*Example*

> *While some people think that environmental health hazards affect only those who work in risky occupations or who live in certain neighbourhoods, it is clear that the problem is more widespread than that. Everyone's life is endangered. Lead, for example, is in the water we drink, the air we breathe, and the food we eat. For Canadians, the likelihood of exposure to serious environmental hazard is now 100 percent, and even low-level exposure to substances like lead can cause serious health problems.*

---

## CHAPTER 7 EXERCISES

1. Write introductory paragraphs, complete with thesis statements, on the following topics:

   a. a habit you would like to break
   b. a book that changed your life

    c.   a hobby
    d.   the effect of technology on your life
    e.   your roommates

2.   Analyze the opening paragraph or so of one of your essays. What introductory techniques are used there? Try rewriting the opening to make it stronger.

3.   Find several articles in a journal related to your area of study. Analyze how these articles have introduced their subjects.

4.   Read the following student paragraphs, all of which served as introductions to essays. Analyze the techniques by which they arouse the reader's interest:

    a.   Any fool can paint a house. A house is comparable to a colouring book — one tries to choose colours that go well together and to stay within the lines. Painting a house needn't be a complicated task; however, some easy-to-make fundamental mistakes can transform your fun outdoor summer project into a nightmare. Let me give you some invaluable advice in the form of three basic guidelines: do not paint a friend's house, do not charge less than $3000, and do not paint the entire house by hand. This sage counsel does not apply to veterans, so if you are already familiar with "The Three Nevers of House Painting" and continue to read, you will not learn anything new.

    b.   I'll let you decide whether I have a problem. Two weeks ago, my roommate Rosella, my friend Dane, and I were leaving to go to a movie. As I was leaving the living room, I noticed the scented candles Rosella had lit and thought, "I'd better extinguish them," and did so. I went to take my shower, and as I was drying my hair, I thought, "Did I extinguish the candles? Maybe I should check, because sometimes when you blow them out, they light up again." I checked the candles for the second time, and then went about my business.

        I checked the candles several more times as I got ready, just to make sure. Finally, Dane arrived and we left. As we drove to the theatre, I began to wonder, "Did I extinguish the candles?" I couldn't remember. I began to envision my apartment building as a towering inferno. About half an hour into the movie, I couldn't take it anymore. All I could think about were the candles. I casually leaned over and asked Rosella if she had checked the candles, to which she replied, "No, I thought you did." I began to doubt myself. I couldn't be absolutely certain that I had extinguished those candles. I got in my car and drove frantically back, listening for sirens all the way. I tore into the parking lot and jumped on the elevator. I ran down the hallway to my apartment. Guess what? The candles were out.

        Recurring thoughts combined with habitual actions are the two main characteristics of obsessive-compulsive disorders.

    c.   Disabled women are perhaps the most underprivileged group in Canada today. As recently as 1985, it was reported that only 4% of disabled women make more than $30 000 a year, and the average salary of the group was $7700 in that year.

    d.   It's a crisp October evening and the crowd roars as the aging star's name is announced over the public address system. He strides confidently to the plate and pauses only to knock dirt off his spikes with his baseball bat before staring down at the pitcher. The batter is a veteran of many seasons and knows what to expect. He bears down and the crowd screams its support. When he goes on to strike out, it seems as though he is the most surprised person in the ballpark. The crowd sighs audibly, and from the back of first base comes the expected cry: "Why didn't you retire years ago, you bum!" Some people just don't know when to quit.

# Drawing a Conclusion

Nothing you write, if you hope to be any good,
will ever come out as you first hoped.
*Lillian Hellman*

Your concluding paragraph is not only your last word on the subject but also an opportunity for you to reinforce your argument. Listed below are four techniques by which you may reinforce your argument in order to end your paper strongly and convincingly. The essay that builds toward a powerful conclusion will not fade out but will reverberate in the reader's mind.

## ■ Retrace Your Line of Thought

Retracing does not mean repeating. Since both you and the reader know where you have been, all you need to provide in your conclusion is a reminder of the steps of the journey. You need only to mention key words that have gathered meaning as the argument has proceeded in order for the astute reader (the one for whom you have been writing all along) to "catch your drift." Echo for effect, rather than for reiteration.

To remind the reader of the inherent structure of your essay, make certain to restate the thesis statement in a conclusive manner, and in different words from those that you used in the opening. Doing so will enable you to check to see if the essay has really lived up to your expectations of it. Keep in mind that the essay is meant to be a lively, though formal, conversation. A subtle reminder of the point you have made will aid the readers; a word-for-word repetition will annoy them.

## ■ Refocus Your Argument

Just as a film director may end a scene by changing the camera focus to wide angle or softening it, so too the essay can take a broader and less stringent view of its subject in its closing.

Widen the focus as you conclude by showing the importance of your topic beyond the immediate concerns of your paper. Beware, however, of writing an overblown conclusion such as "Milton is the world's greatest poet." Instead, include a suggestion for change or perhaps a solution to the problem you have so carefully outlined in the core of the essay.

## Encourage Response

While the body of your essay requires you to provide answers and to be clear and definite in your thinking and wording, there is *some* room in the conclusion for you to mention tentative ideas, to pose questions, or to offer challenges to the reader. You shouldn't open the floodgates too widely, but it is a good tactic to provoke a response in your reader, provided it is relevant to the topic in question. Beware, though, of starting something you cannot finish, or of introducing a topic that sounds suspiciously like what your essay should have been about.

## Make Your Words Resound

By the time you reach your conclusion, you should feel that no important argument for your thesis statement has been neglected. This attitude of confidence will allow you to end your paper with a bang rather than a whimper (to invoke, or rather invert, the words of T.S. Eliot). Make sure that the tone conveys a sense of finality, a sense that you have done all that can be expected within the precise bounds of your thesis statement. The conclusion should not, of course, make grand claims that your essay cannot substantiate.

## Drawing to a Close: Tactics for Ending the Essay

When you come to the end of your essay, consider one of the following ways of formulating a conclusion. Suppose, for instance, that your paper is about the dangers of pollution:

### 1. Decide that enough is enough.

If you find you have nothing pressing to add, say nothing. Make sure, however, that your argument ends on a strong note. Don't stop writing just because you are tired, though.

*Example*

> There is nothing that we do, nothing that we eat or breathe, that does not contribute to the state of our planet, and therefore to environmentalism.

### 2. Take the wider view.

Examine some of the broader implications of your thesis and the questions it may have raised.

*Example*

> As you read through this paper, you probably thought of some things you can do to make your contribution to the preservation of the environment. Although some of these solutions may involve giving up a few of your comforts, you have probably realized that we can no longer blame the other fellow and do nothing ourselves. The poverty, pollution, and poisoning were caused by all of us and can be eliminated only with everyone's co-operation.

## 3. Reinforce your claim.

Remind the reader gently of your line of thought and reiterate your thesis in a slightly different form.

### *Example*

*We are all affected by pollution, but just as we are part of the problem, so we can be part of the solution. Remember these guidelines: reduce, reuse, recycle, and rebel. Reduce the use of electricity and fuel. Reuse things, rather than automatically disposing of them. Recycle refillable containers made of glass, paper, and metal. And rebel by encouraging the government to back tougher legislation to protect our environment.*

## CHAPTER 8 EXERCISES

1. Read and discuss the following conclusions:

   a. It is naïve to assume that Canadian farmers can compete in world markets with a cool climate and accompanying lower yields, as well as higher labour and fuel costs. The protection of Canadian farmers is in the national interest, to ensure the country's food supply and to guard it against pressures that could be brought to bear by such sectors as environmental standards or foreign policy.

      At a time of escalating demand on Canada's food-producing resources, identifying and managing high agricultural land has never been more important. Conversion and loss of agricultural land, particularly prime farmland, to expanding urban land use has diminished croplands and affected environmental quality in North America. With less prime agricultural land available, greater reliance on marginally productive land will occur, and farming these lower-quality areas will be more energy-intensive and expensive.

   b. Computers today, though primitive compared to what will undoubtedly come, are already bridging the gap between human vagueness and computer precision, allowing comfortable interaction. Most computers are now able to run software that lets the user simply point to the function he or she wants to use without knowing complex commands. Many software packages contain on-line help, thus eliminating the need for large printed manuals. And then there is the vast world of educational and entertainment software. With computers one can learn languages, obtain help with algebra problems, or act out the role of any imaginable character in games that are often as complex as movies. Computers are now part of the whole social fabric: they act as the backbone of multinational corporations; they tirelessly tutor a child with his math problems. As technology makes using them easier than ever, computers will gain acceptance by people who once viewed them as intrusive and alien.

   c. In sum, Russell feels that the study of philosophy has had a profound effect on our world. Through its study, a person can free himself from the prejudices of the practical man, and from his physical and biological needs. For Russell, philosophy surpasses the physical sciences it created and is not constrained by the use of measurement, time, and bias. The Self is enlarged through its study and is freed from the constraints of the prison-like world it inhabits, and people will benefit from this freedom. Philosophy exhibits the vastness of the universe, of the mind, while demonstrating the union of the two, and that, according to Russell, is its highest good.

# Writing Paragraphs

> I am convinced that all writers are optimists whether they concede the point or not. . . . How otherwise could any human being sit down to a pile of blank sheets and decide to write, say two hundred thousand words on a given theme?
>
> *Thomas Costain*

Though an essay may not be, strictly speaking, a work of art, it does offer infinite opportunities for the artistic development of your material. What follows are some suggestions on how to develop your paragraphs and how to check to see that paragraphing in the final paper is unified and coherent.

A paragraph must be about one thing. This principle of unity should be so clear that you could compose a heading for each paragraph if the assignment demanded it (and some may).

Logical connections within each paragraph must also be clear. Leaps in logic or unstated assumptions are flaws in your argument that will affect the coherence of the final paper and lose your reader's good will.

Each paragraph is a small step in your total argument, meant to lead the reader onward through your thought process. Hence, each small part must contribute to the whole pattern. Remember that each small section of your argument, each paragraph, is in fact a miniature model of the essay structure itself.

Each paragraph, like the larger essay, should contain the following elements:

1. a topic sentence that reveals the controlling idea, or thesis
2. support related to the topic sentence
3. unity of focus
4. a smooth transition to the next paragraph

## The Topic Sentence

A typical paragraph in an essay begins with a topic sentence, a general "umbrella" statement that explains what the rest of the paragraph is about. Anything that does not relate to this controlling idea should be left out. Sometimes, writers feel that it is unprofessional to make the topic sentence too obvious, but despite their fears, a clear topic sentence is an asset. Because the essay is, by its nature, rather repetitive in structure, you may be simply repeating, in different words, a point that you previewed in your thesis statement. For instance, your thesis statement may be that triage is an essential, if difficult, part of a good health-care system because it enables medical teams to decide which patients must be attended to first. In your first paragraph, you have defined the term "triage." In the second paragraph, you might begin by stating that one of the criteria for setting priorities for care is the patient's chance of survival. Your next paragraph might begin with a topic sentence that mentions the next criterion: the patient's ability to wait. Each of these criteria would be developed in turn.

A topic sentence need not necessarily begin your paragraphs, but for less experienced writers, and in essay writing generally, it usually does.

## ■ The Support

Your support may take several forms:

1. examples
2. statistics
3. connected reasons/definitions
4. authorities

Approach the undeveloped arguments in your outline with these four categories in mind. The sources of support will depend on the nature of the assignment: a formal research essay may require all four; a less formal paper will rely chiefly on reasons and examples for its strength.

## ■ Developing Support for Your Paragraphs

Remember, as you weave your outline into paragraphs, that each discrete unit must ultimately contribute something to the illustration of the essay's thesis statement. The paragraphs argue in its defence or show its validity.

Some of the following methods are formal adaptations of techniques of argument you may have used before. The list is by no means complete; try to think of other equally effective battle plans.

### Present the facts of the case

These facts should include enough to give the reader the point you are making. This indirect opening gives us enough background to recognize that the main point of the paper is the writer's admiration of Chandler's detective character, Phillip Marlowe.

*Example*

In reality, I don't want to be like Phillip Marlowe, the hard-boiled private eye protagonist of Raymond Chandler's detective novels. Marlowe leads a lonely life, solving murders and cases involving missing persons while concomitantly smoking and drinking to excess. He gets brutalized, brutalizes others, and rarely sleeps. His is not exactly the way of life that dreams are made of. Now and then, though, it would be fun to be like Marlowe. His unique, albeit negative way of looking at life is based on his instinctive honesty, indeed an honourable characteristic. Also extraordinary (and let us not forget that this is the world of fiction) is Marlowe's ability to judge, whether a situation or a character. Marlowe, a perceptive "shamus," seems always to make the correct assumptions in a split second. His wit is quick, almost as quick as his right hook or his .38 snub-nose revolver. Whichever of the *three he resorts to, it is inevitably the appropriate weapon. Marlowe is what used to be called a man's man, the epitome of "cool," and drifting off into sleep at night or staring out the window during a class, I'm just like him.*

## Show and tell

To keep the line of thought going, remember that it is always best to argue by example, rather than by precept. Don't just tell your readers about something. Show them, wherever possible, how your idea works by giving an example.

### *Example*

*Admirers of Marlowe know that detective work comes easily to him: he is a natural, like a bee to pollen. Unlike other great private eyes such as Thomas Magnum, who claims to have a little voice in his head forewarning him of danger, Marlowe dismisses the idea of innate ability. Instead, he pokes fun at the simplicity of his business. In* Playback, *he says that tracking a suspect is as easy as "spotting a kangaroo in a dinner jacket." Others may need a little voice or some other instinctive capacity, but to Marlowe, the sleuth business is nothing to be taken too seriously. Of another suspect, he comments, "Even on Central Avenue, not the quietest dressed street in the world, he looked about as inconspicuous as a tarantula on a slice of angel food."*

## Establish connections

Find something in the point you are making that relates to your own experience or to that of your readers. If the essay is formal rather than informal in tone, adapt this advice to show the readers why the subject is important to them.

### *Example*

*Sitting alone in a dusty old office with your feet up on the desk, waiting for business which comes on the average of once per week, sounds very unappealing. Described in such fashion, it is unappealing. The mind of Phillip Marlowe, however, reverses the situation. He realizes the dull nature of his existence at times, and manages to perceive it differently, entertaining himself and those who follow his exploits. His quick wit is not always directed at others. Often, he aims it at himself: "I was breaking in a new pair of shoes on my desk that morning when Violets M'Gee called me up." The long, drawn-out process of labouring over an essay at my own desk has never seemed as cumbersome since I read that passage from* The Lady in the Lake. *I thank Marlowe for that.*

## Define your terms and use details

If the terminology is clear, don't bother telling your readers what they already know. If, on the other hand, you think that a closer look at a word or phrase that is part of your topic will help your case, draw their attention to it.

### *Example*

*Marlowe is a unique individual in his modesty, composure, and outlook. Even a hangover is a new experience as he describes it. After drinking too much whiskey in* The Big Sleep, *he tells us that he awakes "with a motorman's glove in my mouth." Marlowe thinks equivocally, playing off our feelings to express another side to a situation. A hangover can be humorous. And a dead body can be commonplace. For him, in fact, it is simply another part of life. It does not faze him. As he says in* The Big Sleep, *"Neither of the two people in the room paid any attention to the way I came in, although only one of them was dead." Marlowe chooses to concentrate* on the reactions to his entrance rather than on the dead body. Indeed, what is the point of becoming excited about death? Nothing is more final and absolute than a dead body, the ultimate instance of a situation that cannot be changed. A dead body offers little to Marlowe: it cannot answer questions directly. In his business, Marlowe cannot afford to look sentimentally at a corpse. Composure is a necessity for his success.

### Call in an expert or cite a source

Convince your reader by turning to an expert for support. Don't expect readers to take your word for something, if the words of a specialist in the area are available to buttress your own. If the person to whom you refer is a respected authority, your argument will be enriched by his or her utterance.

*Example*

---

This tribute to Phillip Marlowe, in reality, is of course a tribute to the remarkable literary skill of Raymond Chandler. It is Chandler's knowledge of human character and perception of life, combined with his ability to communicate through Marlowe, that created the character I so much admire. Phillip Marlowe is an extraordinary man, but all things considered, I'm glad I'm who I am. Besides, Marlowe would never wish he was somebody else. As Chandler writes, "down these mean streets a man must go who is not himself mean, who is neither tarnished nor afraid. The detective in this kind of story must be such a man."

Note that the source of this quotation would have to be acknowledged, using some consistent form of documentation — a subject covered in detail in Chapter 14.

## ■ Unity

A paragraph, like the essay itself, should have demonstrated the development of your thought by the time your reader finishes it. Each paragraph should lead the reader along in a logical and coherent manner. If your outline has been well planned, the progress of your thinking should be orderly, and your conclusion clear. Your paragraphs should each form a discrete unit, and each paragraph should be clearly connected to what precedes and to what follows.

*Example*

---

It is interesting that beets are rarely offered in these frozen dinner simulations. Possibly that is because beets stubbornly insist on having a beet-like tang no matter how they are diced, sauced, or otherwise adulterated. Such a renegade authentic flavour might take the targeted "average consumer" by surprise. He or she might then realize that the other items on the slab are pale imitations of the real thing. Since that realization could have dire consequences for the manufacturer's cash flow, only cooperative vegetables grace the microwaveable plastic tray.

In this example, the author discusses the quality of vegetables normally used in frozen dinners, by pointing out one variety that never appears. The paragraph then goes on to offer a theory for the beet's conspicuous absence, one that connects this paragraph to the overall notion of the lack of flavour found in frozen dinners.

# ◼ Pinning the Pieces Together — Transitions

Despite the basic structural independence of the paragraph, the reader must be able to appreciate how it fits into the whole essay. To make the connections clear to the reader, an essayist must use appropriate transitions and linking devices.

Transitions are signals of a turn in thought. They often pose a problem for the novice essay writer simply because our methods of changing or developing the subject in conversation are much less formal and much more spontaneous than in written, rhetorical form.

Ask yourself what your favourite techniques of transition in speech are. Then try to categorize the situations that prompt you to use them. You may find that your list of transitions includes such statements as "And you know what else?" to add to or elaborate on a point; "You see," to explain in greater detail; "Sure, but," to disagree with another's argument, at the same time conceding to some degree; "What if . . .?" to put forward a hypothesis; "Anyhow," to dismiss the view of your interlocutor; or "As I said before," to reinforce an earlier point.

Many of these transitions cannot be easily transferred to the printed page. They are too casual to suit the public occasion of the essay. In their stead, the writer must become familiar with and use more formal transitions to enhance the power of his or her rhetoric.

Transitions have many uses. Here are some examples of various transitions:

TO ADD
and
also
in addition
furthermore
as well

TO ILLUSTRATE
for example
for instance
in other words
that is

TO QUALIFY
often
generally
specifically
usually

TO CHANGE DIRECTION
but
however
conversely
although
whereas

TO ENUMERATE
first, second,
first, next, last

TO SUMMARIZE
to conclude
in short
finally

TO DRAW A CONCLUSION
hence
therefore
as a result
consequently

TO ESTABLISH CAUSE
because
for

Good transitions are like carefully sewn seams. Although not readily notice-able, they are the means by which the garment is held together. Shoddy work-manship in your transitions may cause your essay to fall apart — an embarrass-ing state for something that is appearing in print and is being presented to someone you wish to impress.

## ■ Checking the Overall Pattern of Your Paragraphs

There are two basic tests for the aesthetic appeal of the paragraph.

One of these is to read the first sentence of each paragraph to check if the line of thought is clearly maintained throughout the entire work. That is, do the sentences themselves act as subheadings to guide the reader through your design? (*Note*: This test assumes that most paragraphs begin with a topic sentence. Sometimes, however, the topic sentence may appear at the end.)

Another test of effective paragraphing involves looking at the length of the paragraphs themselves on the printed page. Is each of them a manageable length? Most paragraphs will have at least three sentences: a topic sentence introducing the theme that follows, some kind of support, and some elaboration of that support. This is a guideline only; occasionally, a one- or two-sentence paragraph is used for effect. Usually, though, it is a sign of poor thought development and insufficient support.

The layout counts too. Break your paragraphs with an eye to avoiding a "choppy" page or one that presents a daunting block of type.

### CHAPTER 9 EXERCISES

1.  Develop a paragraph using your own definition of a term. Compare it with the definition you find in the dictionary. Try one of these words:

    experience            trial
    determination         misery

2.  Develop a paragraph using a statistic or a quoted authority as support. Look through newspapers or weekly magazines for topics, or try these:

    the state of the economy      the status of women
    educational reform            physical fitness
    the use of computers          a scientific breakthrough

3.  Write a paragraph establishing a connection or making a comparison. Develop your own comparison, or work with one of these:

    video vs. movies          anger vs. rage
    fast food vs. cooking      social drinking vs. drinking as a coping
                               strategy

4.  Develop two paragraphs, one using a real example and one using a hypothetical example. Find your real example in the newspaper or in a magazine, and make up another on the same subject. Try one of these subjects:

someone who is rescued
someone who is guilty
someone who is victorious

5. Write two paragraphs, one using a series of small examples to make a point and one using an extended example to support the same point. Pick any one of these:

how to antagonize a teacher          how to get a good night's sleep
how to flunk out                     how to lose friends
how to start an argument             how to impress a stranger

# Paraphrasing Sources and Integrating Quotations

*It is the little writer rather than the great writer who seems never to quote, and the reason is that he is never really doing anything else.*

*Havelock Ellis*

Not all essays will demand that you use sources other than your own imagination and general knowledge of the world. Many essays, however, will include, as part of the requirements, a knowledge of background sources, all of which must be acknowledged to avoid charges of plagiarism.

Source material, while often a significant part of the essay, does not speak for itself. Remember that the function of paraphrased and quoted matter is to provide support for your arguments. You are responsible for the use you make of the source material. Not only must you be accurate in your representation of it, but you also must be prepared to use it thoughtfully to support your viewpoint.

When you find an idea or a quotation in another source, you are obliged to inform your reader of its origins, even if it is an idea that you already had yourself. Except for the classroom, which is usually considered common domain, the sources of your ideas must be listed in your papers. If you are in doubt about whether or not to include a source for some particular information, put yourself in the reader's place. Would he or she ask, "How do you know this is true?" If so, you need to mention the source.

Quotations and paraphrase are used as support in rather different ways. Quotations are most often used in an essay dealing with literature or a book review, where the main trustworthy source of information is the text of a work itself.

Paraphrase, on the other hand, is used when the exact words are not as important, but the facts they present are; hence, paraphrase is the most common method of using source material in the social sciences. If you find that you must refer to a theory or to an explanation of the meaning of some data, the best plan is to paraphrase. Remember, as you take notes, to paraphrase rather than to quote, taking special care with statistics and their implications.

When you paraphrase some part of a book or article for inclusion as support in your essay, try to get at its meaning. Try to rephrase the thought as if you were teaching the material to someone. Make notes with this principle in mind, taking care to "boil down" the facts and reduce them to their simplest terms, without distorting them. Focus on the thesis statement, topic sentences, and key words, and don't let yourself get bogged down in details. Think the words through rather than just copying them.

Both quotations and paraphrase are used to support your arguments. When you select material from sources, consider the use you intend to make of it. None of the sources will speak for itself; you must demonstrate how a source relates to the case you are building. For this reason, you should usually introduce source material and comment on its function in your paper, rather than assuming the reader will make the necessary connections.

## ■ Borrow Only What You Need

Borrow words, phrases, and sentences only if they add something essential that you do not already possess. Among these essentials are **credibility, power,** and **eloquence**.

The quotations that follow are taken from Michael Hornyansky's brilliant essay "Is Your English Destroying Your Image?" in *In the Name of Language!*, ed. Joseph Gold (Toronto: Macmillan, 1975).

### Credibility

Quote to improve credibility by citing a respected and recognized authority. Or use the quotation as a target for attack, to illustrate that the source itself is doubtful and the object of your critical scrutiny.

### *Example*

*The CBC's newsreaders, once modestly reliable (meaning they could be counted on to apologize for errors), have lost their supervisor of broadcast language and now commit cheerfully such barbarisms as "It sounds like he's going to reform."*

### Power

Quote to demonstrate the power you have at your fingertips, but only to the extent that you will use the quotation. A carefully integrated quotation will show the reader that you have made yourself at home with the sources you have used. Your work will then illustrate your power to cut through trivial details to find the point that demands attention.

### *Example*

*Not all change is progress. Some of it has to be resisted, and when possible reversed. If the last ditch needs defending, I'll take my place alongside Samuel Johnson:*

> *If the changes we fear be thus irresistible, what remains but to acquiesce with silence, as in the other insurmountable distresses of humanity? It remains that we retard what we cannot repel, that we palliate what we cannot cure.*
>
> *(Preface to the* Dictionary)

## Eloquence

Quote rather than paraphrase when no rewording could ever hope to recapture the obvious eloquence of the original writer. Bear in mind that these instances are rare.

### *Example*

*As Samuel Johnson observes, "languages are the pedigree of nations."*

## ■ Begging, Borrowing, and Stealing

In order to avoid accusations of theft, a writer, when quoting, must acknowledge a debt to a source. Don't interpret this to mean that you must quote whenever you borrow. When you paraphrase or when you make reference to an idea, you will also admit your indebtedness. Quote only when it is rhetorically the best tactic: that is, when it adds credibility, power, or eloquence.

Technically, you have not stolen an idea as long as you document its original occurrence. Failure to acknowledge a source is illegitimate borrowing, or plagiarism.

Legitimate borrowing takes place when a writer makes sparing use of some source material by fitting it carefully in the body of his or her essay, without altering it or distorting it in a way that would upset the author.

Avoid borrowing quotations in such a way that the original meaning is changed or even contradicted. The classic example of this shifty tactic is the movie review cited in an advertisement. It may read, for example, "stunning . . . amazing . . . not to be believed," when what the reviewer really said was, "A work stunning in its ignorance, amazing in its clumsy handling of the script, and not to be believed when its advertising describes it as the movie of the year."

## ■ The Fit, Form, and Function of Quotations

The quoted material must fit. It must relate directly to the point under discussion, and it must say something significant. Although quoting often seems like a form of pedantic name-dropping, that is not its rightful purpose.

The function of the quotation is usually to illustrate a point that you have already made in your own words. Bringing in an authority on the subject does not, after all, prove anything; it simply shows your awareness of the position of the experts, whether they be on your side or against you.

The form of the quotation is often the most difficult part of essay writing for the novice. Wherever possible, weave borrowed material unobtrusively into the body of your paper, rather than simply tacking it on.

### Tacking quotations on

While it may be a relief to stop writing and turn over the responsibility for illustrating your thesis to an authority, proceed with caution. Stopping in the midst of a sentence to introduce someone else (usually with a grand and unnecessary flourish) will diminish your own authority as writer.

When you quote, you must remain on the scene, controlling the situation, rather than giving the floor to someone else. Remember, at all times, that the essay is *your* work. When you quote, do not withdraw completely as if another speaker has been hired to do the job for you.

If you have been in the habit of employing long quotations from your source material, try this experiment with one of your past essays. Read the material through quickly. Do you find yourself skimming over the quoted material, or worse, skipping it altogether? Imagine what effect this kind of reading will have on an essay that depends heavily on outside authorities to make its case.

## Weaving quotations in

Wherever possible, make quoted material part of your own sentence structure. This tactic is more difficult but worth the extra effort. First, it will ensure that your reader cannot so easily skip those sections of the paper. Second, it will probably force you to cut quoted material down to the bare essentials, to look at it more closely, and to think of its direct relation to your own thought.

### Example

> When a mechanic reports that "she's runnin' real good," it takes a pretty stuffy professor to reply that "it is running rather well."

To make this technique work to its fullest advantage, there are some rules to keep in mind.

1. Use an ellipsis (. . .) to indicate words that have been left out. But never use ellipses in a way that misrepresents the original. Ellipses are permissible only when you are making cosmetic changes (such as omitting a connective structure that would not make sense out of context). Keep in mind that you do *not* need ellipses at the start of a quotation, even if you did not include the beginning of a sentence in what you quoted, and remember that four dots are used when the omitted words come between two sentences. In other cases, only three dots are necessary.

### Example

> Hornyansky comments that "in our democratic, colloquial society you are more likely to be censured for using no slang. . . . But of course there are risks in using it too. . . . argot that suits one milieu may draw sneers in another."

The original reads as follows:

> I would repeat that in our democratic, colloquial society you are more likely to be censured for using no slang at all. But of course there are risks in using it too. Some sober groups may find your flip ways unacceptable; argot that suits one milieu may draw sneers in another.

2. Use square brackets (even if you have to add them in black pen) to indicate words that you have added. Usually, you will need these only to indicate small cosmetic changes (such as changing a pronoun to a noun or changing

a verb tense to make it consistent with the rest of the verbs in your sentence). Occasionally, you may need square brackets to add a word or two to clarify the context of the quotation.

## *Example*

*Hornyansky addresses "third and fourth-generation Canadians who . . . [speak] English (sort of, you know?)."*

The original reads as follows:

*For I teach third- and fourth-generation Canadians who have spoken English (sort of, you know?) since the crib, yet who have no more sense of English idiom than a recent arrival from the Old Country.*

3. When you use a complete sentence to introduce a quotation, follow it with a colon. Otherwise, use a comma or whatever punctuation you would use if the quotation marks were not there.

## *Example*

*On the subject of pretentiousness in grammar, Hornyansky remarks, "A question like 'Whom do you mean?' really deserves the answer it gets from Pogo: 'Youm, that's whom.' "*

4. Make the terminal punctuation of the quoted material serve your purposes, rather than those of the original. In other words, if the quotation appears at the end of your sentence, close it with a period, even if a comma or other punctuation was used originally.

## *Example*

The original reads as follows:

*For he knows that grammar varies inversely as virility; and that if you continue on down to the stadium, you'll find that nobody there plays well.*

Your paper will read this way:

*Hornyansky believes "grammar varies inversely as virility."*

5. Quote exactly. Do *not* distort a quotation, accidentally or deliberately. The first offence is carelessness, the second fraud. If you detect an error of spelling or grammar in the original, you may tell your reader that it is not your mistake by following it immediately with the word [sic] (in brackets as shown). This notation will tell the reader that the fault is not yours.

## *Example*

*Hornyansky cites the Hon. John Turner's advertisement "in a British newspaper that his four children require a 'kind and loving nannie [sic].' "*

6. Use single quotation marks for a quotation within a quotation, as in the preceding example.

7. Indent passages of prose that are longer than four lines and passages of poetry longer than two lines. When you indent, quotation marks are no longer necessary.

## *Example*

Hornyansky insists on the importance of developing one's own writing style:

> A man at the mercy of his own style is as comic, and as much to be pitied, as a man at the mercy of drink. Your style ought to express what you are, and you are not the same person on all occasions, in every company. If you seem to be, you are a bore.

8. When you have gone to the trouble to quote a source, use it. Explain it, remark on its significance, analyze it, do something to show what it contributes to the whole paper. Don't assume its importance is self-evident.

9. Use quotations sparingly. The essay is meant primarily to present *your* views on a given subject.

# PART FOUR

# Writing the Essay

# Finding Your Voice: Modes of Essay Writing

> The essayist . . . can pull on any sort of shirt, be any sort of person, according to his mood or his subject matter.
>
> *E.B. White*

Role playing is a vital part of the skill of essay writing. You must write the essay confident of your role as an expert. In this chapter, we will modify the general principles of essay writing according to the various purposes of different types of essays, and describe a role you might adopt as the author of one of these types. In addition, the chapter emphasizes the kind of reader or audience that each of the different essay types has. All of the types described share the general characteristics that we have already discussed:

1. a narrow thesis statement
2. a clear outline
3. carefully delineated patterns of argument
4. a unified structure — introduction, body, and conclusion
5. a coherent approach to the integration of support materials
6. an attention to sentence structure, emphasis, and tone

Remember that many of the steps involved in writing the different types of essays described in this chapter overlap. But whether an essay is meant as an informal discussion or as a formal research paper, the steps outlined above are essential. No less important are the steps in revision described in Chapter 19.

This chapter will show you how to prepare yourself for certain specialized types of essay writing. Consult it for advice geared to the particular task at hand.

## ■ The Expository Essay

> You shouldn't pay very much attention to anything writers say. They don't know why they do what they do. They're like good tennis players or good painters, who are just full of nonsense, pompous and embarrassing, or merely mistaken, when they open their mouths.
>
> *John Barth*

The expository essay is the most common essay assignment. It is based on the premise that you learn best about something by trying to teach it to someone else. In other words, the expository essay asks you to play the role of teacher, by presenting your chosen material according to your sense of its meaning and structure.

The expository essay exposes: it shows your approach to a particular subject. As in all essay writing, you must develop a general topic into a specific thesis statement, you must prepare an outline, and you must determine the patterns of argument appropriate to your discussion. The expository essay is different only because its object is primarily to *teach*, rather than to persuade, to present research material, to review, or to express personal conviction.

There are four stages involved in writing the expository essay:

1. Finding your focus
2. Planning your structure
3. Adjusting your level of language
4. Testing your results

These stages, while much the same as those outlined in the sections on developing, designing, and drafting the basic essay, are all affected by your role as teacher, and hence they need special consideration.

## ■ The Role of the Expository Essay

Before you begin, try to see your task in terms of its audience and its purpose.

AUDIENCE: a curious, but uninformed reader, whom you address in a professional but approachable way

PURPOSE: to present some important idea in a way that clarifies it, shows your attitude toward it, and answers questions the reader might have

With these criteria in mind, you can now adjust the stages in writing to suit the occasion.

### Finding your focus

1. Find a subject that you know something about and are genuinely interested in, if possible.
2. Establish your objectives. Like a teacher, you should know what you want your reader to learn from your work.
3. Limit your subject to what can be thoroughly explained within the word length of the assignment. What you propose to show or explain is, in this case, your thesis statement.

### *Example*

| | |
|---|---|
| **Subject:** | *Forest-fire management* |
| **Objective:** | *To show how it is done* |
| **Limitation:** | *The step-by-step process of forest-fire management: prevention and control* |

## Planning your structure

1. Break down the parts of your subject clearly in an outline.
2. Choose the pattern(s) of argument that will allow you to explain most clearly.
3. Connect the steps in your thought logically and clearly.

## Example

| | |
|---|---|
| **Pattern of argument:** | *Process: how forest fires are managed* |
| **Breakdown of ideas:** | *Rough outline* |
| **Thesis:** | *The Ministry of Natural Resources every year sets in motion a regular plan by which to combat forest fires that threaten to destroy Canada's natural resources.* |
| **Body:** | *The Ministry does several things to control forest fires:* |

*1. it establishes central locations where fire fighting begins*
*2. it predicts what areas are most endangered and maps these areas in detail*
*3. it monitors weather conditions and keeps records of soil moisture and amounts of precipitation*
*4. it monitors weather predictions*
*5. it uses aerial patrols and lightning towers to keep watch*
*6. it mobilizes fire crews when fire or smoke is reported*
*7. it dispatches water bombers and erects fire camps in crisis situations*
*8. it supplies all types of fire-fighting equipment*

| | |
|---|---|
| **Conclusion:** | *Fire fighting in Canada's forest regions is a careful process, dedicated to ensuring the protection of precious natural resources.* |

## Adjusting your level of language

1. Keep your reader's level of knowledge in mind.
2. Define all terms likely to be unfamiliar to the reader.
3. Make language concrete, concise, and clear.

## Example

**Level of knowledge:** Provide enough background in the introduction so that the reader will know why forest-fire management is important.

*In 1996 alone, despite preventative measures, a total of 1356 forest fires ravaged 371 358 hectares of prime timber.*

**Use of terms:** Explain terms like "water bombers" and any other terms unlikely to be familiar to a reader.

*A water bomber is a large and cumbersome government-owned plane that can douse a fire with 5400 litres of water.*

**Concrete, concise, clear language:** Tell what a fire fighter does, rather than what fire management is in the abstract. Include plenty of detail.

*Maps that show area landscapes precisely enable officers to see what sort of timber may be threatened by forest fires and what buildings, such as summer cottages and outpost camps, are in immediate or anticipated danger.*

### Testing your results

1. Check your work to see that it is as clear as possible. Put yourself in your reader's place: would you learn from the essay?
2. Have someone else read your work to see that it is readily understandable.
3. Proofread carefully to see that your writing does justice to your thoughts.

## ■ The Persuasive Essay

> No man would set a word down on paper if he had the courage to live out what he believed in.
> *Henry Miller*

The persuasive essay aims at convincing the reader of the truth and validity of your position. Its subject matter is controversial, its thesis one view of the issue. Your task is to win your reader over with your credibility, your wealth of support, and your good reasoning.

Unlike the expository essay, which simply aims to *show* the reader something, the persuasive essay, by taking one side of a controversial issue, aims to *convince* the reader.

Prepare the persuasive essay according to the following stages:

1. Study the issues
2. Pick a side — your thesis statement
3. Make a case for the defence — your support
4. Consider opposing viewpoints, and qualify or refute accordingly
5. Test your argument for fairness and effectiveness
6. Direct your argument, first in outline, then in final form

A persuasive essay may or may not demand that you engage in extensive research to support your case. It does, however, demand that you keep your writing role in mind.

## ■ The Role of the Persuasive Essay

Tailor your essay to fit its special demands.

AUDIENCE: readers who have not made their minds up about a controversial matter and who are willing to make a fair and impartial judgement

PURPOSE: to convince them that your informed opinion on a particular subject is the best one

With these points in mind, consider the stages of the persuasive essay. Suppose you are writing a paper on the accessibility of health care. Research is not a major requirement; what is required is your independent, well-formulated viewpoint regarding this controversial subject.

## Studying the issues

Before you take sides, you must examine all the angles of the question. Make a list of pros and cons about any issue that must be decided or possible answers to any question that must be settled.

### *Example*

**Issue:** *Should the government continue to influence the distribution of physicians across the country in order to improve health-care access?*
*PROS*
*— health care should be accessible to everyone*
*— rural areas are underserviced; most specialists are located in cities*
*— rural areas often lack hospital services*
*CONS*
*— doctors, particularly specialists, must be near hospitals*
*— the financial constraints of building and maintaining hospitals in rural areas are overwhelming*
*— the cost of health care itself impedes access to it*

## Picking a side

1. Choose the side for which you can muster the most support. If possible, choose a thesis that you genuinely believe in.
2. Define your position by making a claim or by arguing against another's claim.

### *Example*

**Side chosen**: *The distribution of physicians has no real bearing on health-care access.*

**Position defined**: *The current distribution of physicians does not affect health-care access. The high cost of health care is the main constraint to adequate access.*

1. *Physicians, particularly specialists, must be near medical facilities to run their practices effectively.*
2. *Physicians, therefore, should not be penalized for their decision to practise in cities, as they have been in Quebec, Ontario and British Columbia.*
3. *The number of physicians should not be increased, as it has been in the rest of Canada, since that "solution" only increases the cost of an expensive health-care system.*
4. *More hospitals cannot be built and maintained in rural areas without increasing expenditures even more.*
5. *The current situation, where general practitioners tend to work in towns and rural areas and specialists choose cities, is the only workable way of balancing cost and access.*

## Making a case for the defence

1. Gather support for your arguments. In some instances, this support will come from books or journals, though it may also come from your own clear understanding of the issue.
2. Use your own reasons, and if research is required, use statistics and expert opinion as further support. Remember to acknowledge sources.

## Example

(Expert Opinion)

*Accessibility is a fundamental principle of Canadian health insurance. The 1966 Medical Care Act "requires insured services to be delivered in a manner that does not impede or preclude, either directly or indirectly . . . reasonable access."[1] In keeping with this principle, both federal and provincial governments have tried to change the geographic distribution of doctors in an effort to correct a perceived inequitable distribution of physicians. They hoped thereby to improve access to health services in rural areas.*

## Example

(Statistics)

*In the 1960s and early 1970s, the federal government attributed the low physician-to-population ratio in rural areas to an overall shortage of doctors in the country. They believed that if there were more doctors rural areas would no longer be underserviced.[2] So, the Canadian government responded to the problem by increasing the capacity of domestic medical schools and opening immigration to physicians. Between 1968 and 1974, the number of physicians in Canada grew by 8151, or 36 percent;[3] however, the distribution of physicians between rural and urban areas remained disproportionate, and the gap even worsened in Ontario.[4] In fact, the growth in the number of physicians increased health-care costs, but it did not improve the accessibility of health services.*

## Example

(Reasons)

*Actually, the increase in the number of physicians to which governmental controls has led is responsible for increasing health-care costs; to build more hospitals would increase these costs even more. Given that funds are limited, if every small town were provided with a fully equipped hospital, then the more expensive equipment and treatments — like CAT scans and cancer treatments — would not be available anywhere in Canada. It might also become necessary to impose restrictions on accessibility similar to the rationing of health care in Britain, where — as a means of containing health costs — kidney dialysis is not available to National Health Service patients over fifty-five years of age.[5]*

## Considering opposing viewpoints

1. Anticipate objections to your arguments as you go along.
2. Treat the opposition fairly.

## Example

**Anticipated argument**: *In spite of these arguments, the number of physicians in rural areas is still smaller than it should be to ensure access to health-care services.*

**Fair treatment**: *a counter-argument that analyzes the problem closely*

*Although rural areas tend to have fewer physicians per capita than cities, the difference in available medical services is not necessarily proportional to the difference in the respective physician-to-population ratios. Family and general practitioners gravitate toward smaller towns, while specialists tend to settle in cities.[6] The significance of this fact lies in the kinds of medical care these doctors provide. GPs perform a considerably wider range of services than do specialists. To some degree, then, one GP acts as a substitute for the many different specialists available in the city, so access to health care may not be as unequal as the present geographic distribution of physicians implies.*

## Testing your argument for fairness and effectiveness

1. Check for fallacies, or flaws, in your argument.
2. Weigh your words carefully, avoiding biased or vague, unconsidered words.

When writing (or reading) any persuasive essay, you may fall prey to a number of logical errors in your thinking. Remember that certain arguments are not in the spirit of fair play. Learn to recognize the following faulty arguments or fallacies and avoid them in your own writing:

**1. Accepting glib generalizations.** An argument that uses catch phrases like "Canadian identity" or "freedom of the individual" in an unthinking way may just be appealing to what the words conjure up, rather than to any thoughtful meaning assigned to them by the writer. Make sure such general appeals can be pinned down to specifics. If the mayor of your city argues that he or she will work to increase "civic pride," ask what specifics such a general statement entails.

**2. Arguing *ad hominem*.** This kind of argument distracts readers from the issue being discussed and, instead, uses personal attacks against an opponent. For example, someone might argue that health-insurance fees should not go up because doctors are interested only in making money. Here the personal charge being made may have nothing to do with the issue.

**3. Establishing faulty cause and effect.** This kind of faulty reasoning assumes that there is a connection between two events simply because one followed the other. For instance, if a political party claims that it is responsible for a drop in interest rates that occurred during its period in office, we need to ask if such a drop might have occurred regardless. After all, there may be many other ways of explaining changes in interest rates.

**4. Making a faulty analogy.** Often we make analogies, or comparisons, in order to show significant similarities between things. We must, however, always take care to make sure that such comparisons are fair. Commercials are often the chief offenders in this regard. Is a day without orange juice really like a day without sunshine? Check to make sure that your own comparisons are appropriate.

**5. Assuming an "either/or" situation.** One of our commonest assumptions is that there are always two sides to any issue. In fact, there may be many more than two sides. See to it that you do not phrase your arguments in such a way that they falsify the problem. It is probably not true that if you don't believe in free enterprise, then you are a communist. Be aware of other possibilities between extremes.

**6. Jumping on a bandwagon.** When you deal with a controversial topic, make sure that you examine the issues carefully before arriving at your own point of view. The argument that something is right because it is "modern," or "current," or "up-to-date," or because everyone is in favour of it, will not stand up.

**7. Begging the question.** You beg the question when you assume the truth of what you are trying to prove. For example, if you argue that books should not be taxed, it is not enough to say that no one could possibly support a tax on books because it will lead to increasing illiteracy. The onus is on you to prove that illiteracy will increase; you cannot simply assume so.

## Example

You may want to argue against this stated position:

> Health-care access would be more equitable if physicians were more concerned with taking care of patients than with making money.
>
> **Checking for flaws**: Look at the underlying biases of the statement.
>
> This statement assumes that doctors practise in cities in order to make more money than they would in rural areas, but no proof is advanced for the claim. Here, in other words, the argument begs the question.
>
> **Weighing your words**: It is important to find evidence to justify any claim that you intend to make. The argument above rests on an unexamined assumption.

## Directing your argument

1. Remind your readers of the points you are making by reinforcing those points as you go along.
2. Engage your readers as comrades-in-arms, not as antagonists. Assume that they are reasonable and open-minded about the issue. Do not assume that they are antagonistic.

## Example

Look at these techniques in the following paragraph, which concludes the paper on access to health care:

> Since every small town does not have a hospital and physicians are not located in proportion to demand, barriers to access to health services unquestionably exist; however, the cost of breaking down these barriers is higher than the cost of their presence. Ultimately, then, it is the cost of health care itself that impedes equal access. With limited government funds, equality of accessibility to health services is little more than an idealist's dream. So far, measures to make such services more accessible have invariably increased costs by more than they have improved access. Policies aimed at changing the distribution of physicians and hospitals are not the solution. Clearly, the federal and provincial governments need to change their approach to the issue of health-care access.
>
> **Reinforcement**: Summary of the line of argument

# Keeping Your Head: Kinds of Essay Writing

## ■ The Essay Examination

> Every writer I know has trouble writing.
> *Joseph Heller*

Essay examinations are frequently a source of panic because they strip the writer down to the bare essentials. Without hours of preparation to cover your flaws, whether in knowledge or fluency, you may feel exposed — unless your work is genuinely in good shape. An essay examination, because of its time limitations, is brief but not without style.

The advice that follows will help you write a better examination, if you approach it in stages:

1. Getting in shape
2. Coping with exam shyness
3. Making the material fit
4. Taking the plunge
5. Standing out in a crowd

## ■ The Role of the Essay Examination

Remember your reader and your aim:

AUDIENCE:   an expert (not an antagonist) who wishes to test your knowledge and facility in his or her discipline

PURPOSE:    to show what you have learned and how you can apply it

### Getting in shape

An examination is only the product. What determines its outcome is your preparation, not only in the nervous hours immediately before it, but in the days and weeks preceding it as well.

To make your performance on the exam less fraught and more predictable, prepare for it gradually. If you have faced your fears throughout the year, the final countdown should not be anxiety-ridden. At least, your conscience will be clear if you have attended class, read the textbooks, and completed the course work.

## Coping with exam shyness

**Analyze the shape you're in.** Be brave. Take a good hard look at yourself. Judge your past performance in the course. Consider the amount of work you have done. If you're already in good shape, this step will increase your confidence. If not, read on.

**Limber up.** Even a well-prepared student will need to warm up for the examination by conducting a review. Review course work by setting up a reasonable work schedule and then following it (with some flexibility, of course).

Review does not mean reread. Review should be refreshing, just as a warm-up exercise is meant to get you ready for more and not to drain you of energy. Review is just part of the routine. Look through your notes and your texts, as well as your past essays and tests. This process will be easier if you have highlighted important points beforehand (and if you have done all the required work in the first place).

**Locate problem areas.** To overcome shyness about the exam, you must confront your fears. Ask yourself, unflinchingly, what are you afraid of? If you find that you are worried about some specific problems in your understanding of the course, pay particular attention to these. The benefits will be twofold: you will conquer some of your fear, and you will learn something.

## Making the material fit

In order to learn anything, you must make it a part of yourself. You must carry it away with you and get carried away with it (while still keeping your feet on the ground).

To gain full possession of the course material, you will use **memory, fluency, application,** and **imagination.** Here's how.

**Memory.** There is no learning without memory, though memory is just the first step in turning course material into something of your own. To sharpen your skills of recall, try reading aloud, so that both sight and hearing can register the information.

Concentrate on facts and significant details. Help your memory along by making associations or by visualizing material. These tactics will trigger memory when you're stuck for words.

If memorizing is not your strong point, don't despair. Although an essay exam demands that you have some facts at your fingertips, how the facts are presented, how they are used, and what you create out of them are equally important.

**Fluency.** To make yourself an expert in a discipline, learn how to speak its language as you master its content. Make the terms a part of your language, by learning to define them, by including them in speech, and by using them in writing. When imagining how you would answer a question, talk to yourself. Jot down notes. The more conversant you are with specialized language in your subject area, the more gracefully you will write under pressure.

**Application.** Make sure you can use what you know. To apply your knowledge, you need to supply a context. Don't just repeat the facts: question the material. As you review, note questions that the textbook may have raised. Keep in mind any questions raised in class or topics distributed for review that strike you as pertinent. These may prove useful when exam time comes.

**Imagination.** All work and no play would make a dull examination and certainly a grim study period. Approach the test and your preparation for it with a sense of play, if at all possible. Wonder about its potential. Don't confine your imagination to the tried and true; experiment with some ideas of your own. Develop a theory or two, as if you were preparing for a formal essay. You may well get a chance to try them out on the examination. The difference between an A and a B is often a desire to develop your own ideas and to create something new out of the material.

## Taking the plunge

Writing an examination successfully depends on two factors: what you know *and* what you can say about it in a limited time. To make the best use of your time, follow this basic pattern: **read, sketch, write, skim.**

**Read the questions carefully.** Before you get your feet wet, so to speak, read over the entire exam. Take careful note of the instructions. If you are given a choice of questions, devote a few minutes to their selection. Allot an appropriate amount of time for each question and *adhere to that schedule*. It is wise to begin with the questions you know best.

Look for questions to challenge you. Remember that an essay question does not necessarily have a correct answer. An essay simply tries, as its name suggests, to come to terms with a provocative, perhaps troubling, question.

Become familiar with these common examination terms:

### *Explain*

If you are asked to *explain*, be thorough in your approach and ready to clarify in detail, as though you were teaching the reader. Both structure and substance are needed, so be prepared to show both breadth and depth in your treatment of the question.

### *Example*

> The federal Progressive Conservative Party has been called the "normal opposition party." *Explain*. What must the federal Progressive Conservative Party do to become the "normal government party"?

Begin by using facts to explain the label "normal opposition party." These facts should be available to you from the course material. Then, making sure to refer to appropriate sources, discuss various theories of what is needed to ensure Conservative success at the polls.

## Discuss

If asked to *discuss*, use the latitude of the question to focus on some part of the problem that captures your attention and allows you to present a lively, informative, and thoughtful consideration of the problem. Treat the question as if you were writing a less than formal essay — as indeed you are.

### Example
---

*Discuss the ways in which family ties and loyalties dramatically expand the inner conflicts and crises of conscience in* Huckleberry Finn *and* King Lear.

Begin by focussing on the conventional bond between parents and children. Show how the bonds are broken in both works. Then you could go on to show how a new sense of family is created for both Lear and Huck in the levelling process that occurs in both works. Remember to include many examples to support your points.

## Outline

If asked to *outline*, put your emphasis on the bare bones of the argument — the facts — rather than the flesh. An outline will require you to place more stress on the shape and the sequence of your subject, rather than the substance.

### Example
---

*Outline how and why geographical factors are so strongly evident in classical mythology.*

Your outline should be broadly based, isolating a number of examples of geographical factors in a variety of myths, rather than in one or two. Follow these examples with a discussion suggesting some of the reasons for this phenomenon. Aim at broad coverage rather than deep analysis.

## Compare and Contrast

If asked to *compare and contrast*, or simply to *compare*, remember that the object is to show the relationship between two things. Focus the essay on the connections and differences you find by setting two things side by side in your sketch.

### Example
---

*Compare and contrast the women's movement of the late nineteenth and early twentieth centuries with the women's movement which began in the late 1960s.*

Begin by making an outline to discover the main similarities and differences. Say, for example, that the main similarities include the desire to change attitudes toward working women and the desire to gain more influence in the workplace. The differences might include the earlier movement's focus on political rights and the later movement's focus on issues relating to sexual harassment on the job. You could compare and contrast not only the goals of the movements, but also the relative success of each of them. Then you need a summary of your findings, in order to compare these two movements more generally.

**Sketch**

Sketch out your answers to the questions chosen. First, let yourself go. Jot things down helter-skelter as they occur to you. Then, try to gather material into categories for discussion. Avoid getting embroiled in outlines too complex or too demanding for the time allowed.

Sketch your answers in the briefest possible form. As you do so, use key words in the question to guide your responses. Above all, obey the terms of the question as you work in the things you want to say.

**Write**

Sketching your material enabled you to get warmed up. Therefore, the writing process itself should be more graceful and more organized. To ensure an organized presentation, fall back on established essay-writing habits. Begin at the beginning. Make sure your answer has an introduction, a body, and a conclusion. While these sections will be hastier and less polished, do not abandon structure entirely.

The main thing to keep in mind is the connections you are making between the question and the knowledge you brought with you into the exam. Refer to your sketch and to the original question as you write, but also allow yourself the freedom of an unexpected idea or a unique turn of phrase, as long as it doesn't interfere with the basic flow of your answer.

Let the words flow, but keep the writing legible. Write on every other line as a courtesy to your reader.

**Skim**

Force yourself to read your answers quickly and to make small changes. To neglect this stage is to force your instructor to become the proofreader — a proofreader who might become annoyed at your carelessness. A small mistake is forgivable; reckless abandon is not.

## Standing out in a crowd

Now that you know how to pass an essay examination, you may well wonder how to surpass expectations. Though you are writing the examination along with perhaps hundreds of other students, there are ways of making your exam style unique without defying the conventions of test writing.

What does a bleary-eyed instructor, marking two hundred essay questions, look for in an answer?

**Definition.** An essay examination is your chance to show your understanding of how some terminology in the subject area works. Unlike a multiple-choice exam, this kind of test will allow you to use the language of the discipline precisely and fluently.

**Direction.** Your answers should be pointed directly at the questions. Don't make the mistake of trying to say everything; you can't assume that the instructor will give you credit if he or she can find the right answer somewhere in your paper. You also can't assume that your instructor will want to look for your answer. Make your answer easy to find.

**Detail.** While even an exceptional student cannot remember all of the fine points in a complex body of work, it is certainly possible to learn a smattering of appropriate details on a variety of subjects. Such details may be inserted, where applicable, as you are writing the exam. Details have the effect of a close-up. They allow you to focus on something precise, and they reveal your careful reading of your subject matter.

**Depth.** To demonstrate depth of knowledge, an examination must show that the writer has thought about the implications of the subject and of the specific question. Dive in. Don't avoid entirely the deeper complexities of a question in favour of its superficial requirements. Where possible, do more than you need to do. Answer questions seriously; you are writing as a curious and concerned expert. Address your subject, not as an illustration of how well you have learned it, but rather as a serious attempt to advance the subject matter itself.

**Discovery.** A brilliant exam will show what a student has learned above and beyond what the instructor has taught. If you have some insight or even some questions about the material that have not been raised in class, this is your opportunity to voice them. Never recite the answer to a question based on your memory of a lecture unless you have, sadly, nothing of your own to add to the material. An exam should occasionally allow you to take intelligent, calculated risks.

## ■ The Précis or Summary

> When you catch an adjective, kill it.
> *Mark Twain*

A précis is a concise summary of a longer passage. Sometimes a précis will be an assignment in its own right; on other occasions, it will be something that you prepare as part of writing a larger essay of your own. The ability to summarize one's own or others' work is important: often, you will be asked to provide short summaries of your written material, whether in abstract form, as is the case with dissertations, or in executive summary form, in the case of reports. Sometimes, too, a précis will provide you with a short memo about what you considered the key features in a work central to your research. The task of writing a précis will help you learn to focus on the line of argument in a passage and will oblige you to reconsider it in your own words; this kind of engagement with source material, or even with your own writing, can be invaluable in honing your critical abilities. In addition, précis writing can help make your writing more concise.

# ■ The Role of the Précis

Before you start, conceive of your task in relation to its audience and its purpose.

AUDIENCE:    someone who wants you to give a quick overview of a detailed piece of writing without sacrificing central content

PURPOSE:    often to reduce a passage to one-third or even one-quarter of its original length, occasionally even shorter, in a way that keeps the original focus and does not obfuscate ideas

Assuming that your task is to reduce a passage to one-third of its original length, you can now follow these guidelines:

## Reading the original passage

1. Read the passage to ferret out its main focus.
2. Try to reconstruct the organization of the passage as you read through it.
3. Jot down the main idea of the passage, and mark ideas that are central to it, or peripheral to it, as you go along.
4. Reduce the passage to an outline that constitutes its line of argument.

## Condensing sentence structure

Many constructions in English are redundant and can be substantially reduced without adversely affecting content. Here are some suggestions about how to reduce the sentence structure you find in a longer passage:

**1. Leave out appositives, words, or phrases that rename other words.**

### Example

*Socks, his cat, caught her third mouse this week.*

*Socks caught her third mouse this week.*

**2. Leave out words that are included only for emphasis.**

### Example

*Bill was very disappointed.*

*Bill was devastated.*

**3. Change figurative language, such as similes and metaphors, or omit them.**

### Example

*Tilly worked like a dog on the project.*

*Tilly laboured on the project.*

4. **Leave out introductory constructions like "It is ... who" or "It is ... which."**

*Example*

It is Cathy who works in the library.

Cathy works in the library.

5. **Find one word that will do the work of several.**

*Examples*

Cole is a man who had once taught school.

Cole is an ex-teacher.

Dil left the room without a sound.

Dil left the room silently.

6. **Find words that allow you to generalize rather than particularize.**

*Example*

Nelly bought hamburgers, french fries, and soft drinks.

Nelly bought fast food.

7. **Turn rhetorical questions into statements.**

*Example*

What kind of person would be interested in yet another situation comedy?

Few people would be interested in yet another situation comedy.

8. **Leave out lengthy illustrations; just stick to the facts.**

*Example*

The Keener can only be described as looking like someone who would own an extensive collection of stuffed toy animals. The Keeners, when not in their professor's office (having him or her grade the first draft of a paper that is not due for three months), can be found sitting at the very front of a classroom or in any section of the library where the "No Smoking" by-law is strictly enforced. These perky students have an unprecedented amount of apparent enthusiasm for even the most dreary topics. It must be admitted though that the educational background of the Keeners remains something of a mystery. Nevertheless, they exhibit a childlike fascination with every idea that is presented to them. As most Keeners have never read a book that was not on a course outline, they do not have a true favourite author, but when pressed for an answer, they respond with, "Probably A.A. Milne, but Watership Down *is one of my favourite books; I really felt for the bunny rabbits."*

Keeners are childlike, perky, and enthusiastic, even about dreary topics. They can often be found in a professor's office or at the front of a classroom. They read only books on course outlines, and their educational background is a mystery.

## 9. Combine short sentences to reduce word length.

### *Example*

---

*In the nineties, more unrelated people are living together under the same roof. These people may be joined together for love. They may be joined for convenience. Or, they may be joined out of necessity. Whatever the reason, choosing a roommate is one of the most important decisions you will make. If two people are united for love, then choosing a roommate is a very personal decision. If two or more people are going to live together for convenience, or out of necessity, then choosing roommates is an important decision. This decision must be well thought out because choosing the wrong roommate could cost you financially, physically, and mentally. Choosing a roommate is difficult, but the process you use in choosing a roommate is as important as the roommate you choose, because the process you choose will lead to your roommate, and your new roommate will have a significant effect on your life.*

*In the nineties, more unrelated people are living together under the same roof, for love, for convenience, or out of necessity. If two people unite out of love, then the choice of a roommate is personal; however, if you live with someone for convenience or out of necessity, you must choose cautiously. The wrong roommate could cost you financially, physically, and mentally. Choosing a roommate, though difficult, is crucial because the roommate chosen will have a powerful effect on your life.*

## Writing the précis

1. Write out in your own words the main points in the passage.
2. Check that words you substitute are appropriate to their new context. Check the precise meanings of words.
3. Keep the original paragraph structure unless the piece is short.
4. Try to keep the tone and style of the original intact.
5. Do not add anything as you interpret the passage.
6. Keep the word length to approximately one-third of the original, unless otherwise instructed, but don't cut out essentials.
7. Read the passage again and revise carefully.

## ■ The Informal Essay

---

All writing is communication; creative writing is communication through revelation — it is the self escaping into the open. No writer long remains incognito.

*E.B. White*

In most cases, the essays you write as part of your course work will be formal in tone. When you are allowed the luxury of writing an informal essay, follow these basic suggestions:

1. Be yourself
2. Choose a comfortable subject
3. Experiment with style and subject
4. Shop around

# ■ The Role of the Informal Essay

The informal essay affords you greater freedom and a more casual approach than the formal essay. Although the same writing process is demanded in the informal essay — it too needs a thesis statement, a typical essay shape, and a command of the mechanics of writing — what you say and how you say it are a matter of invention rather than convention.

AUDIENCE:   friendly company who find your perspective stimulating

PURPOSE:   to talk about anything that appeals to your imagination

## Be yourself

The informal essay should let the reader learn about you and about your subject. Whereas you are obliged to keep a restrained and professional distance in the formal essay, you should maintain a casual and personal tone in the informal essay. Someone reading your paper will learn not only the facts and figures of your subject, but also some of your characteristics and your attitudes.

You will necessarily be more exposed: flaws in your arguments, biases in your attitudes, and unattractive aspects of your personality may show. The informal essay is by definition a face-to-face meeting between you and the reader. To prevent excessive vulnerability, you must examine your attitudes scrupulously, and be prepared to face your reader's reaction — alone.

## Choose a comfortable subject

Whereas a formal essay must be logical, objective, tight, and well supported, an informal essay allows you to be more subjective in your viewpoint, more personal in your selection of supporting material, and more idiosyncratic in your approach.

The formal essay may argue a life-and-death matter; the informal essay is, by contrast, an intellectual exercise for its own sake. This characterization does not mean that the informal essay cannot be heartfelt or deeply important — but its tone is less public, its argument closer to your personal interests, and its value less dependent on knowledge of facts than on grace and eloquence.

## Experiment with subject and style

You must draw the material and the viewpoint from your own sense of the subject, rather than looking to authorities for defence.

In an informal essay, your object is to keep your reader interested in what you have to say. You cannot assume that the subject is intrinsically appealing to the reader from a professional standpoint, as you do in the formal essay. Since the material you choose in the informal essay reflects you and your personal understanding of the matter, you must appeal to your reader personally and share your opinions enthusiastically.

The informal essay allows you the opportunity to experiment with language in a way that would not be appropriate in a formal or research essay. Try writing as you speak — without lapsing into grammatical and structural errors. For example, in an informal essay, you can use contractions (don't, can't, etc.), which are generally not acceptable in a formal essay.

## Shop around

Make an effort to read some personal essays, whether newspaper editorials or in magazines or the "collected works" of a classmate. Here are some choices for stylistic study:

| | |
|---|---|
| Ellen Goodman | Allan Fotheringham |
| Harry Bruce | Joey Slinger |
| Michele Landsberg | Lewis Thomas |
| Russell Baker | Barbara Amiel |
| Fran Lebowitz | James Thurber |

## CHAPTER 12 EXERCISE

Read the following informal essay and answer the questions that follow.

For many years my mother was an active leader in the Girl Guides of Canada. Each year, planning the annual camp kept her busy from spring until midsummer. Her arrangements included finding a cook, a nurse, a lifeguard, and a lifeguard's assistant. By the time I was about fifteen years of age, I had qualified as the assistant and would go off with her to "do my duty" on the banks of the brown/ green pond at Camp Dahinda. My duty, besides ensuring the safety of youthful swimmers, involved swimming in the wake of a rowboat which was propelled by the lifeguard around the perimeter of the pond each morning. It seemed like a strange ritual, but as it was a part of my job I never questioned its necessity. In retrospect, I have decided that the title of assistant lifeguard was a glorified designation for human bait; the pond was infested with leeches. I now believe that, primarily, I was responsible for drawing as many of the bloodsuckers out of the pond as could be attracted during a half-hour swim! This process would ensure a reduced population for the campers who would be swimming later.

My equipment list for those camping trips included no more than dry clothing, a couple of bathing suits, several towels, and a full saltshaker; salt is used to disengage a leech from skin.

It was during these back-to-nature stints that I started loosely categorizing campers, according to attitude and equipment, into three groups: survivalists, quasi-campers, and those who, like myself, are interested in escaping from the world of telephones and in finding easy access to an affordable retreat. I hadn't consciously given this last category a name, but I suppose we could be called "the poorly paid."

Beginning with the survivalist variety of camper, we find the guy who lives to test himself against the natural world. The survivalist spends much of his civilian life in subtraction, carefully eliminating non-essentials from his list of things to take along on forays into the wilderness. His motto echoes Darwin's: "survival of the fittest." His objective is to fuse with nature — to rely solely on his survival instincts for endurance in no man's land for at least a couple of weeks each year. Though he does admit a few basics to his inventory (groceries and some form of shelter), a true survivalist harbours a private longing: to test his mettle in the wild with only the clothes on his back, some string, a fishing hook, and a container (perhaps a hat) in which to place nuts and berries.

I have a friend who fits nicely into the survivalist group. Tim likes to hike the Bruce Trail every year. For weeks before he sets out, he haunts a local army surplus store, shopping for freeze-dried groceries and other camping curios that will double his pleasure when it comes to hardship. To some degree, this is a sensible exercise. Whatever goes into his pack must be carried on his back for a predetermined distance every day. Buying easily prepared, lightly packaged food is judicious. Nevertheless, sometimes I think he carries "roughing it" a bit too far. For instance, one year he came in and tossed a handful of chemicals and a canteen on my kitchen table. He proceeded to explain: "If I were to swim out into the lake a little way and fill my canteen with water, I could then produce water fit for human consumption just by adding these chemicals." He exhaled a long indulgent sigh when I asked, "Why not just fill the canteen with water from the garden hose outside the shops where you buy your cigarettes?" I knew the answer to this question before I had asked it — the garden hose method would be too easy.

Tim's portable water treatment plant reminded me of a scene I had witnessed years earlier at one of my mother's Girl Guide camps. A group of six girls, would-be survivalists to be sure, were preparing their evening meal. Two were bent over a pile of leaves and twigs diligently whirling sticks back and forth between their palms, and intermittently striking bits of flint together, all to no avail. A half dozen feet away, two others were opening cans with a can opener. It occurred to me that if you could compromise with cans and a can opener, instead of foraging for assorted natural ingredients, then why not just toss on a lighted match to start the fire? A third pair of Guides, whom I will call the fly swatter shift, were vaulting around a picnic table, smacking every winged thing within reach. The activity of this last pair of girls completed an incongruous picture when juxtaposed against the young pyromaniacs who were still unsuccessful in their quest for fire. Indeed, the exterminators were definitely in way over their heads from a survivalist's perspective. After all, isn't camping all about being in harmony with the natural world as you find it — including the acceptance of insects? As someone who has once earned her keep as human bait, and who attracts not only water-bound pests but the airborne variety, I feel compelled to come to their defence.

In my estimation, acceptance or non-acceptance of the insect population is one area that defies a perfect separation between categories of campers. Though pest control is a practice unthinkable for the true survivalist, the other two groups labour to execute this task with zestful devotion. For the most part though, the crossover between quasi- and poorly paid camper ends with the cold-blooded dedication to insect genocide.

Aside from conquering the insects, the challenge of the quasi-camper seems to lie in transforming the natural world into an illusory suburbia. The quasi-camper is the person who backs a forty-foot mobile home onto a site and spends the next several hours hooking up all his gadgetry before nightfall. The quasi-camper is not really curious about nature and has no real interest in camping. His mania lies in technology and in things portable. His aim is to bring as much civilization to nature as he can sustain on wheels. On board, he has all of the comforts of home: air conditioning, full bath and shower, refrigerator, microwave, propane barbecue, and always, a colour television with VCR and remote control.

Until a year ago, when I visited my sister at the Pinery Provincial Park, the notion of putting a mini house on wheels and driving into the woods for a couple of weeks was inconsistent with my idea of camping. However, I have changed my mind; there is something to be said for a few luxuries.

My sister Mary and her husband, Mike, do not seem to fit into a specific category of camper. They are survivalists in the sense that if they manage not to kill themselves while camping, then they have accomplished what they set out to do. Yet they are quasi-campers in desire, and poorly paid in practice.

Last year, when I arrived for lunch, Mary was bustling around hanging all of their sodden gear in trees while Mike was busy trying to chase a sizable body of water out of the tent with a broom. The campsite that they had chosen was lovely, though, unfortunately, it was a sort of bowl-shaped area. They had raised their tent in the deepest depression on the site. In the predawn hours, they had been all but washed away in the torrential rain that had heralded the start of a new day.

After we had put the camp into some sort of order and re-established the tent on higher ground, we salvaged enough food from the items floating around in the cooler (their ice had melted) and made lunch. Then we set out in the van to drive to one of the nature trails in the hopes of photographing some of the deer that wander at will through the park.

Mike explained that, if we were to see any deer, we would have to refrain from loud conversation. Though we were all very quiet, we never did see any deer. I think it might have had something to do with the slapping sounds punctuating the stillness at periodic intervals. None of us had remembered insect repellant; our walk had quickly deteriorated into a sort of calisthenic hat dance as we tried to defend ourselves from millions of ravenous mosquitoes.

The deer continued to elude us as we drove back at breakneck speed toward the campsite. I did catch sight of a brown blotch in a stand of trees once, but at the rate we were travelling, I had difficulty focussing.

That day at the Pinery was a good one; it inspired me to do a little camping myself. And, as I seem to embody the true spirit of the poorly paid, I offer myself as an example of the final category. Unlike the survivalists, the poorly paid plot to leave behind the business of everyday survival; such activities become routine in the workaday world. Therefore, they will take along not only the necessities, but a few frivolous things to make the holiday more pleasurable. On the other hand, indulgence is restricted by budget; anything extravagant that is not already in one's possession, and not absolutely portable, must be left behind.

For my own camping holiday, I borrowed a tent and started compiling a list. Since my microwave isn't portable, I made sure that breakfast was cereal; lunch I could skip, as is my habit anyway; and for dinner — well, hot dogs would save washing dishes in the evening. Once the menu was complete, in order of importance I packed insect repellant, a coffee maker (I was going to spring for hydro), something in which to keep fresh water (of the hose variety), basic toiletries, some bedding, my camera, a flashlight, batteries, some books, pen and paper, and a Scrabble game. And then I was ready, for this is the stuff of which the poorly paid camper is made.

1. How is word choice used to enhance the humour of this essay? Find examples to support your point.
2. How is each of the three categories of camper illustrated?
3. Examine the introduction and conclusion. How is each of these made effective?

# ■ The Literary Essay

> Real art has the capacity to make us nervous. By reducing the work of art to its content and then interpreting that, one tames the work of art.
>
> *Susan Sontag*

The literary essay requires you to read, to analyze, and to come to terms with the meaning of a piece of literature. Whether it demands secondary sources or simply focusses on the literary work itself, the literary essay demands that you show your understanding of how and why the work is put together the way it is.

Write the literary essay according to the following stages:

1. Formulate a thesis about the work
2. Read the work closely
3. Use secondary sources, if required
4. Select only the best supporting evidence
5. Quote often, but not at great length
6. Write in the present tense
7. Write with both the text and the argument in mind
8. Revise with style

AUDIENCE:    someone who has read the novel, or poem, or short story, but who wants to understand more about how it works (for example, its structure, its themes, its techniques)

PURPOSE:    to interpret the meaning of a work and the techniques by which that meaning is revealed

## Formulate a thesis

The thesis of the literary essay should be something that helps the reader make sense of the work in question.

For example, in the essay that follows on p. 91, the reader needs to know what accounts for the new popularity of musical theatre. The student's view of the question is her thesis: that musicals are now popular because they capitalize on the audience's longing for escapism and they can appeal to great numbers of people, beyond national boundaries.

In Joseph Conrad's *Heart of Darkness*, the reader needs to know why Conrad includes the passage in which Knights, the first narrator, and Marlow, the second narrator, discuss the Thames river. Your viewpoint on this question will determine your interpretation of the work's meaning.

Find your thesis by asking yourself what the important questions are about the literary work you have in front of you. Sometimes these will be assigned, but sometimes you will have to find your own questions, based on class discussion and reading.

Remember that you cannot conclusively prove your thesis statement. All you are expected to do is to show that your reasons for it are based on the text itself.

## Read the work closely

With your working thesis in mind, read the work carefully. Underlining or highlighting the text as you go along is often a good idea (provided you own it, of course).

Note anything that might count as evidence for your analysis of the characteristics of a literary work. Don't, however, neglect passages that might support a contrary view. You will need to account for these as well.

## Use secondary sources, if required

Maintain your balance when using secondary sources. Use them to get some critical perspective on the work in question, but remember that your own task is no different from theirs. The main reason for writing a literary essay is to show your own powers of analysis.

Keep track of the sources you have consulted. The ideas you find must be acknowledged to avoid charges of plagiarism. Keep track also of the basic line of argument set forth by each critic you consult: it is unfair to take ideas or phrasing if you intend to use them out of their original context.

## Select only the best evidence

After close reading, you need to "back off" from the work somewhat. Your task is not to summarize the work, or to explain every detail of it, but merely to present a viewpoint that suggests what the work means and how it is put together.

Skim through the work, noting down the most prominent support you have found. Then, categorize the material into sections appropriate for discussion in your essay. Fit these into a rough outline, and you are ready to write.

### *Examples*

1.  *Thesis statement: Musical theatre is now thriving in Canada because of an audience eager for spectacle and escapism and because producers can appeal to a mass international market.*
    A.  *Musicals are now very successful in Canada.*
    B.  *Nostalgia and spectacular stage effects are reasons for their success in bad times.*
    C.  *Musicals transcend national boundaries and so are lucrative but perhaps not socially aware.*
2.  *Thesis statement: Conrad includes the discussion of the Thames so that the reader will become aware of the effects of conquest on the conquered as well as the conquerors.*
    A.  *Knights sees the Thames as symbolic of the light of civilization; Marlow sees it as symbolic of savagery.*
    B.  *Knights is romantic and patriotic about England's empire; Marlow calls to mind ancient times when England was conquered by the Roman Empire.*
    C.  *Knights, like the readers, modifies his view of the Thames in response to Marlow's narrative.*

To stress that the two narratives are meant to parallel the readers' change in perspective as they read, the last point focusses on the alteration in Knights's view of the river near the end of the work.

As you gather support, try not to include everything. Pick only those passages central to an understanding of the work's meaning and those that work best as illustrations of your thesis.

## Quote often, but not at great length

The best illustration of a point in a literary essay is a quotation. Whereas paraphrase may be a useful way of reporting research, the quotation is the most precise way to examine meaning in literature. Exactitude is important.

Remember, though, that you must *use* your quotations. Don't just copy them and assume that your point has been made. Focus in on them to show exactly how they work as support for your thesis. Don't assume that the meaning of the quotations or your purpose in quoting them is self-evident.

## Write in the present tense

When discussing a work of literature, stay in the present tense — treat the work as a living thing.

### *Example*

*Knights describes the river in romantic terms.*

History, on the other hand, and accounts of historical events, are written in the past tense.

## Write with both text and argument in mind

Stay close to the text and to your argument at all times. But remember that you are not writing to record the plot or to state the obvious. Assume that the reader has read the work. Your job is to offer an interpretation of its meaning. Use the primary text to *demonstrate* your thesis and present your support for the argument at every step of the way.

Write an analysis, not an appreciation or a summary. Don't, for example, waste words admiring Sondheim's skill as a lyricist or Conrad's skill as a novelist. Instead, show how a particular literary work is put together and explain why it has the effect it does.

Assume that the work has unity and coherence, unless evidence shows otherwise. Take the text apart and show how some features of it work. Your job is to show how its synthesis is achieved.

When you are not working with a literary text alone but are instead analyzing a phenomenon, such as musical theatre, remember to keep your focus on the argument and your support for it.

## Revise with style

In a literary essay, style is crucial. Your grade will depend not only on what you say but also on how you say it. Check for grace in style. Aim at writing smoothly and confidently. Find a critic you admire and emulate his or her method of proceeding. Your argument, no matter how cogent, will not succeed unless your paper is written well.

The following are sample literary essays whose format conforms to the new MLA guidelines. Refer to the section Documenting — MLA, APA, and University of Chicago Guidelines, pp. 125–140 for more information. Study it carefully, noting the format and the method of documentation.

— Pages are numbered in upper right-hand corner (omit number on first page when title page is used).

Lorna Phillips

Popular Culture 100

Professor Desai

12 March, 1997

Crazy for Musicals:

The Success of Spectacular Theatre in Bad Times

— Omit this information when title page is used.

Musical theatre, in spite of high costs for both its producers and its audience, is now, once again, a prominent part of popular culture and often an enormous financial success. This comparatively recent change in the fortunes of Canadian theatre is in part due to the emergence of an audience eager for spectacle and escapism and to producers' abilities to appeal to a mass international market.

It is certainly clear that the musical is a thriving form of theatrical presentation. The large amounts of money spent on their production, the long runs that many popular musicals enjoy, the increase in theatre building in Canada, at least in centralized areas, and the vast sums spent on merchandising items such as compact discs, T-shirts, posters, and glossy programs all attest to the proliferation of this form of entertainment. Broadway hits like Miss Saigon and Crazy for You demanded an initial investment of $10 million and $8.3 million dollars (U.S.) respectively (Weber C15). The Canadian version of Miss Saigon is itself a $12-million production (Bemrose 34). — References made in parenthesis are followed by page numbers.

The commercial success of musicals in cities like Toronto can be shown by the high degree of entrepreneurial involvement in their production. David Mirvish, to accommodate his production of Miss Saigon, an established hit since 1989, built the Princess of Wales Theatre, "the first privately built hall for live theatre to be erected in Canada in almost 90 years" (Bemrose 34). The triumph of that musical in London, New York, Tokyo, and Chicago assures its ability to secure large revenues in Canada and thus to support Mirvish's investment in the theatre.

— Enclose short quotations (fewer than four lines) in quotation marks and include them in the body of the essay.

Nor is the success of <u>Miss Saigon</u> an isolated phenomenon. David Mirvish's father, Ed Mirvish, owner of Honest Ed's in Toronto, was himself a wealthy businessman turned theatre owner. He went from a warehouse business designed "to sate rampaging middle-class appetites for everything from Hula Hoops to TV dinners" ("Expectations" 92) to the ownership of Toronto's Royal Alex and Britain's Old Vic. No longer just a businessman finding ways to profit from consumerism, the elder Mirvish is now considered to have made "a permanent contribution to Canada's cultural life" (Jenish 28). One can also point to the great financial fortunes of Garth Drabinsky's production in Canada of <u>The Phantom of the Opera</u> or to the even more lucrative example of <u>Les Misérables</u>, which sold 4.5 million tickets in Canada, making it the most successful musical in Canadian history (Bemrose 34). Indeed, the producers themselves see these shows as unabashedly commercial enterprises, though some critics have seen them as evidence of what is disapprovingly called "commodity theater" (Bentley 281). Cameron Mackintosh, the British co-producer of <u>Miss Saigon</u>, admits to the flashy production values and the commercial appeal of the show when he claims, "if <u>Les Misérables</u> is a Cadillac, then <u>Miss Saigon</u> is a Ferrari" (Bemrose 10). His analogy of the musicals to flashy cars demonstrates the importance of stunning production values and extravagant visual appeal. Both the cars and the musicals are meant to impress with their looks and their cost.

To understand why such flamboyant and financially staggering shows have reached a pinnacle in difficult economic times, it might be useful to draw a comparison with a similar situation in the Victorian era. Michael R. Booth, in <u>Victorian Spectacular Theatre 1850-1910</u>, argues that there is a "relationship between spectacle, realism, historicity, archaeology, and pictorialism" (29) that accounted in large measure for Victorian theatrical concerns. The Victorians, he claims, were interested in recapturing the past and in seeing the world that was increasingly open to their curiosity. Just as now, Booth acknowledges that spectacular theatre was seen as carrying "the

Underline book titles in essay and in list of works cited.

taint of vulgarity and tastelessness" (29), but nonetheless, it was popular and had its origins in the tastes of the times.

Nostalgia and the desire for spectacular stage effects, as in Victorian times, coupled with bad economic conditions, have led to the success of the musical in recent years. As Morley writes,

> Musicals enjoy a boom in a period of economic recession. . . . An audience that has trouble finding the money for its tickets is also keen to see how the money is being spent, and musicals with huge sets and lavish costumes fulfil an economic and escapist need. They also pose no real challenge: in the case of a revival, where one can actually go in humming familiar songs, the public can also be reasonably sure of what they are buying in advance at the box-office. (220)

Musicals, in other words, are a sure thing, a recognizable and generally a happy representation of life that comforts the audience and delivers the expected goods for the purchase price.

As in Victorian times, too, the emphasis on the pictorial may be accounted for by an increasing sense of participation in the larger world. Victorians, fascinated with exotic foreign places and with remote times, demanded a stage that could reproduce them. These days, with so much money at stake, as British critic Sheridan Morley remarks, "a successful record plus a Broadway deal, and if possible a film option as well, are needed months if not years before a first night" (210). To make money, spectacular musicals must appeal to the wider world and not be constrained by national concerns. Media involvement is obviously a prerequisite of financial gain. And such involvement often transcends national borders, allowing for the growing import of British and American productions. Not all critics are happy about the turn that theatre has taken as a consequence of media salesmanship. Robert Wallace, a Canadian theatre critic, writes, for example, that national theatre will suffer as a result:

> now that commercial theatres are producing foreign work with the economic backing of international corporations — not to mention major

*Use an ellipsis to indicate words omitted.*

*Indent long quotations (four or more lines) ten spaces; omit enclosing quotation marks.*

financial support by all levels of government in the case of the Elgin and

Winter Garden theatres — the strength of this competition has increased

enormously. With millions of dollars to market their products and

palatial theatres in which to present them, companies like Cineplex

Odeon have changed the face of Canadian theatre. Their high profile in

the media and the marketplace — Phantom is "co-marketed" in ads for

Pepsi Cola and American Express — works to redefine what Hans Robert

Jauss calls the "horizon of expectations" that an audience brings to the

theatre. (54)

This tendency, Wallace effectively argues, works against anything but central,

urban, mainstream theatre financed by multinational corporations. It may,

consequently, silence the voices of groups without that kind of financial

backing or that kind of access to the world marketplace. It may result, he

argues, in a homogenized theatre incapable of providing expression to

marginalized ways of thinking. Such an international and corporate

domination of the theatre may also be hurtful to Canadian nationalism:

> In the minds of many people, productions like Les Misérables and The
>
> Phantom of the Opera confirm an idea of theatre that much indigenous
>
> Canadian work has tried to disestablish during the last 20 years:
>
> namely, that theatre is a special, expensive "event" — a product of older,
>
> more established cultures that Canada must import and enshrine in
>
> lavish institutions deemed appropriate to its revered status. (Wallace 54)

Wallace's point here is that theatres should not be seen as institutionalized

corporate bodies that sanction certain attitudes, but should instead challenge

the minds and the societies in which they find themselves. Indeed, Swain

argues powerfully that the popular tradition of musical theatre would benefit

from critical attention that attempts to explain its aesthetic effects (7).

Despite their capacity to evoke former times and thus appeal to nostalgic

yearnings, musicals are not always frothy productions devoid of social

conscience or artistic acumen. One need only think of Stephen Sondheim's

Sweeney Todd, which Morley terms "an angry musical about blood and death

and social corruption" (203), and Willy Russell's British musical <u>Blood
Brothers</u>, considered a "marvellously tough, grainy, black show" (203), to
realize their potential to affect the emotions of their audiences to social ends.
Even classic novels like <u>Jane Eyre</u> have been recently given musical treatment,
in a form that tries to do justice to both emotional and narrative complexity.
Musicals, like film, provide modern audiences with an opportunity to revisit an
old love in a new shape, and the Mirvishes' stage production of <u>Jane Eyre</u>, like
Zeffirelli's film version, offers new perspectives that are not necessarily
simplifications. Yet it is also true that the most profitable shows are frequently
those that transcend national barriers and hence, often social concerns, like
<u>Cats</u> or <u>The Phantom of the Opera</u>, whose main appeals are clearly spectacular
and escapist.

Works Cited

Bemrose, John, and Diane Turbide. "A Home for Miss Saigon." Maclean's 24

    May 1993: 34.

Bentley, Eric. The Playwright as Thinker. New York: Reynal & Hitchcock, 1946.

Booth, Michael, R. Victorian Spectacular Theatre 1850-1910. London:

    Routledge & Kegan Paul, 1981.

Braun, Liz. "Putting on a Superior Eyre." Toronto Sun Apr. 26, 1996: 17.

    On-line. 17 Jan. 1996.

"Great Expectations." Canadian Business Sept. 1988: 92.

Jenish, D'Arcy, and Brian Willer. "The Lights, Sound and Action of a

    Community Man: Edwin (Honest Ed) Mirvish." Maclean's 25 Dec. 1989: 28.

Morley, Sheridan. Spread a Little Happiness: The First Hundred Years of the

    British Musical. New York: Thames & Hudson, 1987.

Swain, Joseph. P. The Broadway Musical: A Critical and Musical Survey. New

    York: Oxford UP, 1990.

Wallace, Robert. Producing Marginality: Theatre and Criticism in Canada.

    Saskatoon, SK: Fifth House, 1990.

Weber, Bruce. "A Crazy Little Thing Called Financial Success." Globe and Mail

    4 Dec. 1993: C15.

List alphabetically by last name.

List only works cited in essay.

Periodical references must include complete page numbers of article when listed in works cited.

Abbreviate publication information without sacrificing clarity.

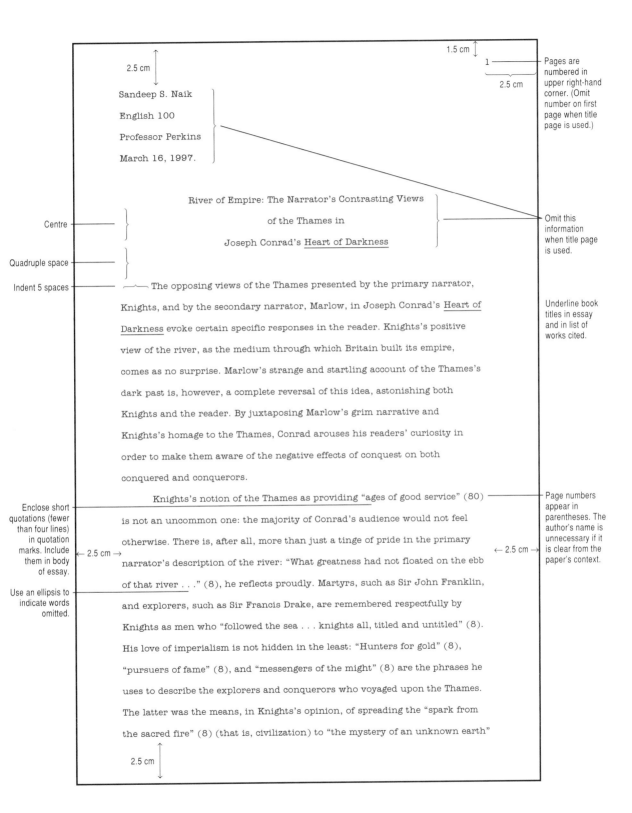

1.5 cm

1

2.5 cm

Pages are numbered in upper right-hand corner. (Omit number on first page when title page is used.)

2.5 cm

Sandeep S. Naik

English 100

Professor Perkins

March 16, 1997.

Omit this information when title page is used.

Centre

River of Empire: The Narrator's Contrasting Views

of the Thames in

Joseph Conrad's Heart of Darkness

Quadruple space

Indent 5 spaces

The opposing views of the Thames presented by the primary narrator, Knights, and by the secondary narrator, Marlow, in Joseph Conrad's Heart of Darkness evoke certain specific responses in the reader. Knights's positive view of the river, as the medium through which Britain built its empire, comes as no surprise. Marlow's strange and startling account of the Thames's dark past is, however, a complete reversal of this idea, astonishing both Knights and the reader. By juxtaposing Marlow's grim narrative and Knights's homage to the Thames, Conrad arouses his readers' curiosity in order to make them aware of the negative effects of conquest on both conquered and conquerors.

Underline book titles in essay and in list of works cited.

Knights's notion of the Thames as providing "ages of good service" (80)

Enclose short quotations (fewer than four lines) in quotation marks. Include them in body of essay.

← 2.5 cm →

is not an uncommon one: the majority of Conrad's audience would not feel otherwise. There is, after all, more than just a tinge of pride in the primary narrator's description of the river: "What greatness had not floated on the ebb

← 2.5 cm →

Page numbers appear in parentheses. The author's name is unnecessary if it is clear from the paper's context.

Use an ellipsis to indicate words omitted.

of that river . . ." (8), he reflects proudly. Martyrs, such as Sir John Franklin, and explorers, such as Sir Francis Drake, are remembered respectfully by Knights as men who "followed the sea . . . knights all, titled and untitled" (8). His love of imperialism is not hidden in the least: "Hunters for gold" (8), "pursuers of fame" (8), and "messengers of the might" (8) are the phrases he uses to describe the explorers and conquerors who voyaged upon the Thames. The latter was the means, in Knights's opinion, of spreading the "spark from the sacred fire" (8) (that is, civilization) to "the mystery of an unknown earth"

2.5 cm

(8), such as Africa. Indeed, without the Thames, the "seed of commonwealths, the germ of empires" (8) could never have been planted.

Marlow's strange and startling account of the Thames's dark past is quite different. The "sacred fire" (8) Knights values so deeply is just "a flash of lightning in the clouds . . . [a] flicker" (9) in Marlow's eyes. To him it is darkness that has prevailed, a darkness symbolized by the Thames. He substantiates this view by presenting the other side of imperialism: the darkness and misery associated with, and inflicted on, the vanquished. It was the Thames that brought the Romans, says Marlow, to a land of "cold, fog, tempests, disease and death" (10), a far cry from the empire it would one day become. There are no Sir John Franklins or Sir Francis Drakes in Marlow's view, only "the utter savagery . . . of wild men" (10). Whereas Knights associates the Thames with calmness, serenity, and tranquillity, Marlow believes it led to danger, evil, death, and destruction: "No Falernian wine here" (10), Marlow says, rejecting the glory and heroism that Knights embraces. For Marlow, there is only "death skulking in the air . . . [men] dying like flies . . . the incomprehensible" (10).

Though vastly different, the opinions of Marlow and Knights are not unrelated by any means. Knights presents imperialism from a romantic perspective, full of the praise and respect he has for his native land. For him, it is the heart of an empire. By presenting this aspect first, Conrad subtly allows the readers to participate in this familiar view. Almost immediately after, though, the readers face Marlow's idea of the Thames as the means by which the Romans were able to capture the "unknown earth" (8) that would one day be Britain. Marlow describes a Thames of "nineteen hundred years ago" (9) when Britain was not the conqueror but the conquered, a complete turnabout of the patriotic perspective, and one unfamiliar to most readers. Conrad exploits this unfamiliarity to change the readers' point of view.

Such a response from the readers is critical to the rest of the novel. From this point on, the readers have questions about the experiences that have led Marlow to see the Thames in this light. This first difference of opinion leads

Use square brackets to add words needed for clarity.

to Marlow's account of his life in Africa amidst "all that mysterious life of the wilderness that stirs in the forest" (10). Marlow's view of the Thames's history also sets the tone for the story that follows: it introduces the contrast between growth and destruction, the conquerors and the conquered, the civilized and the savage, and of light versus darkness.

The readers, like Knights, are affected by Marlow's view of the Thames and by the narrative that follows. In the end, Knights sees the Thames in a changed light: though still "leading to the uttermost ends of the earth" (76), the river now "flowed sombre under an overcast sky — [where it] seemed to lead into the heart of an immense darkness" (76). By using the double narration, Conrad has created a character in Knights whose response to Marlow's account of the Thames, and to his story, serves as a guide to our own. In this manner, Conrad manipulates us in the hope that Knights's newfound awareness of the price of imperialism is also our own.

Works Cited

List according to last name and in alphabetical order.

List only works cited in essay.

Conrad, Joseph. Heart of Darkness. Ed. Robert Kimbrough. 3rd ed. New York:

Norton, 1988.

Abbreviate publication information without sacrificing clarity.

# The Book Review

Most of the book reviews you will be asked to write have a more specific purpose than the kind you see in newspapers and magazines. You will be asked not only to report on the content of a book and to evaluate it, but also to analyze it in terms of its contribution to the discipline. A book review gives you a chance to examine one potential source in a given area, often as a prelude to writing a research essay. Like any other essay, it demands a thesis statement that clarifies your reaction to the book.

If you are asked to review a book as part of a course requirement, select a book with a subject matter that appeals to you and with which you feel comfortable. Proceed according to the following stages:

1. Describe or summarize the contents of the book
2. Describe and evaluate its tactics
3. Consider its contribution
4. Illustrate your argument
5. Maintain your critical balance

To write a focussed book review, remember your role as fair-minded and helpful critic.

## The Role of the Book Review

Like other essays, the book review's form is determined by its readers and its function.

AUDIENCE:    someone who has not read the book, but who is interested in its subject matter and has some background in the discipline

PURPOSE:    to summarize, analyze, and evaluate a book, and to show your critical acumen in so doing; then, to recommend, to criticize, or to dismiss the book according to careful judgement

### Describe the book

1. Determine the thesis of the book (if it is a critical text), the theme (or general meaning) of the book (if it is not), and the audience for which the book is intended.
2. Summarize the book's contents briefly, without giving the show away.
3. Use the book's preface, introduction, and table of contents as a rough guide for your discussion of the work.
4. Discuss the general purpose of the book, without getting caught up in too much detail.

___

*Neil Postman, in his book* Teaching as a Conserving Activity *(1979), argues that the function of formal education should be to counteract the biases of the culture, rather than to reinforce them. To illustrate this point, he focusses on the pervasive influence of television and other media and recommends that education teach society to be more critical of the media. Postman intends this book to be a modification of his earlier work,* Teaching as a Subversive Activity *(1969), in which he advocated innovation. In this book, his argument is that education must work against the unthinking forces of change that prevail in the culture as a whole.*

## Describe and evaluate the book's tactics

1. If the book is a critical text, describe its method of argument. If it is not a critical text, describe the techniques by which the material is presented.
2. Note how well the book does what it sets out to do.
3. Note what else might have been done or what might have been done differently.
4. Note why you liked (or disliked) the book.

*Example*

___

*The book sets out to show how television has affected our way of seeing the world. It argues that television has made us less conscious of the past, that it has lowered our attention span, and that it has made us more susceptible to "quick-fix" solutions to problems — as a consequence of too much exposure to television commercials, which reduce life to shallow and easily remedied problems.*

*Postman insists that the way to counter this problem is to teach people about the media and about how the media alter our perceptions of things. He argues that the development of strong critical-thinking skills will put a stop to the passivity and superficiality of the cultural attitudes provoked by television viewing.*

*The chief flaw in Postman's approach is his own lack of sources. Given that he advocates critical appraisal of the means by which information is conveyed, the onus is on him to show that some of the effects of television that he lists are, in fact, present.*

## Consider the book's contribution

1. Compare the book to others you have read with a similar thesis or theme.
2. Ask yourself what you learned from the book.

*Example*

___

Teaching as a Conserving Activity *seems to present a useful corrective to the problems of value in education today. Postman points to some real dangers created by the commercialization of the media and emphasizes the role that education must play in maintaining old values in society as well as espousing new ones.*

## Illustrate your argument

1. At every step of the way, use snippets from the book to back up your position and to give the reader a taste of the work.
2. Include both positive and negative illustrations, unless, of course, your review is entirely positive or negative (rarely the case).
3. Be sure to integrate your illustrations from the book as part of your argument, and not simply as decoration.

## Example

*Although some of the charges Postman makes about the negative effects of television are justified — such as its invasion of privacy and its stress on seeing things from the outside, superficially rather than analytically — some of his charges are exaggerated. When he claims that television is not analytic because it is "picture-centered,"[1] he argues that we cannot prove a picture true or false the way we can a proposition. But Postman here is comparing apples and oranges. Words are not always used to create propositions either; sometimes they tell stories, just as pictures do, and these stories cannot be categorized as being true or false either. The fault, if there is one, does not lie with the medium, but instead, perhaps, with the use to which it is put. In other words, television in itself does not automatically lead to a deterioration in critical-thinking skills.*

## Maintain your critical balance

1.  Don't be intimidated by ideas just because they are in print. Your object is to assess the merits of the book in question.
2.  Don't be too harsh in your judgements. Remember that the author deserves mercy as well as justice.

## Example

*Ultimately, Postman's position that education should move to counteract some of the biases of the culture is a valid one: some of his arguments for it, however, need more support and closer critical scrutiny than he has given them.*

---

## CHAPTER 12 EXERCISE

Read the following book review and analyze its structure, using the questions that follow:

Moonbeam on a Cat's Ear by Canadian author/illustrator Marie-Louise Gay is a highly recommended addition to any collection of children's literature. In 1987 it was awarded a well-deserved Amelia Frances-Howard Gibbon Medal from the Canadian Library Association. Aimed at the preschool audience, the text is sparse and characterized by slight rhyme, and the illustrations are rounded, colourful, lively, and detailed. Specifically, Moonbeam on a Cat's Ear is the ideal bedtime book for children, and the illustrations and text are integrated with this purpose in mind.

Like the large-bodied, broad-faced, tiny-limbed characters in her other books (Lizzy's Lion, Rainy Day Magic, Angel and the Polar Bear) who embark on amazing journeys before returning to reality, Rosie and Toby Toby awake from their beds and journey through the sea and sky on the moon with a cat and a mouse before they return to their beds and sleep.

All of the action in the story is carried by the illustrations. The pictures show a strong substory not necessarily indicated by the text. The story begins by describing the illustrated scenes of the sleeping cat, then switches as Toby Toby enters Rosie's room and entreats her to go on an adventure. As Toby Toby begins musing about their plans with increasing excitement, the pictures show the characters actually doing the things he describes. This process escalates to the point of the characters being in the sky surrounded by lightning bolts, when Rosie says, "Oh Toby Toby it's so frightening!" The next page shows them both asleep on the bed. At this point the text asks a direct question of the child:

> Was it a dream
> or did they really try
> to steal the moon right out of the sky?

As the illustrations show a stronger story than the text (just as the imagination is sometimes stronger than reality), the question posed is answered for the child by the final illustration of the cat and mouse still seated on the moon in the sky. Flipping back to the previous page confirms the animals' absence from the bedroom.

Through her use of such ambiguities, Gay reveals great insight into the minds of children. She omits adults from the story and focusses directly on the problems facing a child being put to bed. Children's bodies are relatively still (like the text), but their imaginations are alive and travelling (like the pictures). When the characters return to earth and are shown sleeping, a sense of calm is produced, but the last picture and teasing question allow something for children to think about as they fall asleep.

The author uses colours and techniques conducive to sleep. The predominant colour in Moonbeam on a Cat's Ear is blue. This, combined with a margin of white space surrounding each page, creates, even in the most active scenes, a quiet mood appropriate for bedtime. Marie-Louise Gay, in an interview with Marie Davis, speaks of the story as a "moon book": "The quietness, the serenity in Moonbeam is also due to the contrast between the bluish light and the stark white light. Everything seems to float in space." She speaks of other ways in which she invokes this mood: "I had tiny little borders, but they're not too intrusive. They have little things happening in them, but they're much calmer, like little paintings" (Davis 81). In painting the scenes, Gay has used a somewhat unusual technique that, while still using bright colours and distinct lines, produces a soft, dreamlike quality. By putting a white paint mixture on the gesso board and letting it dry with brush strokes in it, Gay achieves a ridge-like texture when she adds ink and watercolour on top.

Gay's use of perspective is cinematic in some respects. The book opens with a close-up of a cat's ear against a night sky, and then on the next page, the viewer sees the cat sleeping on the bed inside underneath a window. The third picture backs off even further, showing the mouse of which the cat is dreaming and Rosie in bed. Next, with a knock on the door, comes a shot of a previously unseen corner of the room, with a close-up of Rosie's startled face on the facing page. The next page shows the distanced darkened shadow of Toby Toby in the open doorway, contrasted in the next frame with a lightened close-up revealing Toby Toby with his flaming red hair and red pyjamas to match. The following two-page frame shows the joined shadowed backs of the figures of Toby Toby and Rosie as they exit out the front door into the night. In order not to disturb the flow, Gay shows the open door of Rosie's bedroom with the emerging figures of the cat and the mouse. The remaining pictures are shown at a middle range. The ninth picture is interesting since it is drawn looking down on Toby Toby as he reaches up from the top of the apple tree toward the unseen moon while the diminished figures of Rosie, the cat, and the mouse look upward. The final picture of the sleeping cat and mouse on the moon is from a distance and is in contrast to the opening close-up of the cat's ear.

Frames are used interestingly in this picture book. Gay's frames span the length of two pages for peaceful scenes and scenes in which the two characters are together. Single-page frames are used for abrupt actions, like the knock on the door, Rosie's startled face, or Toby Toby's darkened shadow. When Rosie becomes afraid in the storm, the picture is continued on two pages, but is split down the middle by the white of the inside margins.

Overspill is also used to dramatic effect. In overspill, illustrators extend drawings beyond their usual confines to provide viewers with a sense of parallel stories and/or additional dimensions. In Moonbeam on a Cat's Ear, the amount of overspill parallels the amount of action in the illustration. The quiet scenes in the beginning contain only a minimal amount of overspill, such as the butterfly wings, the tip of the moon, or the edge of the pillow. The extension of Toby Toby's hair over the border emphasizes the text below the picture, "with the bright red hair." As Rosie and Toby Toby go outside, their shadows in the doorway extend outside the frame to the bottom of the page. Change in lighting in Gay's work represents a change in the tempo of a story, a graphic depiction of what is happening inside the mind of a child. Because of the importance of the shift of the pictures away from the text in this story, a high degree of overspill exists. The overspill becomes more frequent as the action continues outside, for example, with the top of the apple tree (to emphasize height), the tips of the grounded moon boat (to emphasize length), the top of the sail, and then the lightning bolts, until the children are back in bed, when the overspill diminishes.

The amount of detail in the text serves many functions. It creates a sense of immediacy or realism. Examples from Moonbeam on a Cat's Ear include the shadows of moonlight, the messy state of the toys, scarves, coats, and shoes, and the open scissors beside bits of paper on the table top. Detail also helps create a sense of movement. In Gay's story, movement is always present, whether in the slight blowing of curtains, the flying of moths or the leaping of fish, the falling off of a slipper, or the streaks of movement behind the lightning bolts or the children as they fall.

The details also enhance the sense of flow and connection in the pictures. The cat and the mouse are present on every page, if one looks hard enough. (So is Toby Toby's frog until it wisely jumps off when they leave the water.) The moon appears on almost all the pages, whether it's in the sky, on Rosie's pyjamas, in the margins, or on the picture hanging on the bedroom wall. Even the mouse, dreamed by the cat, dreams himself of little cheese moons. Likewise, lightning bolts accompany the knock on the door; they are on the wallpaper, in the margins, and in the sky. The airplanes on Toby Toby's pyjamas are also found in the margins; the bed sheet turns into a sail, then back into the bed sheet again. Detail can enhance the flow of the story in even subtler ways, such as in the repetition of the shape of the cat's ear in the curtains or in the butterfly wings.

The detail in the borders has a more formalized structure. The tiny pictures help the flow of the words and alert the viewer to related details in the bigger illustration. When Toby Toby is high in the tree, there are images of rockets and kites in the margin. When the moon-boat leaves the sea for the sky, fish are shown leaping amongst clouds. The borders reinforce, but they also foreshadow. On the first page, the sequence of the phases of the moon is shown in the border. Apples are shown on the border of the page before the apple tree is shown. The cat and the mouse peek around the picture in the border of the page before they are shown sleeping on the moon on the last page.

This examination of Moonbeam on a Cat's Ear suggests some criteria for deciding a book's place in a collection of children's literature. One may want to consider Canadian content or medals awarded. One may also want to ponder intended audience, purpose, or message, and how well that purpose is achieved. The colour and quality of illustrations are important. As well, the integration between a text and its illustrations is vital to the coherence of a story intended for children. Here, technical issues like detail, style, innovation, consistency of scale, arrangement of text and pictures, flow, length, and readability come into play. The author's understanding of children and their interests is crucial if a picture book is to reach its intended audience.

1.   How does the essay show the integration of text and illustrations?
2.   What kinds of support does the essay writer use?
3.   Analyze the strengths of the introduction and conclusion.

# ■   The Research Essay

> I write in order to attain that feeling of tension relieved and function achieved which a cow enjoys on giving milk.
>
> *H.L. Mencken*

A research paper is a formal essay based on your exploration of other people's ideas, rather than simply an analysis of your own thoughts. Although both the expository essay and the persuasive essay may use source material to some extent, the research essay is unique. Its purpose is to formulate a thesis based on a survey and assessment of source material.

The following steps are essential to the development of a research paper:

1.   Mapping out the area of exploration
2.   Finding a working bibliography
3.   Drawing up an outline
4.   Recording source material
5.   Writing and documenting your essay

# ■   The Role of the Research Paper

A research paper must be modified to suit its readers and its special aims.

AUDIENCE:   an informed, curious reader, whom you address on a professional level

PURPOSE:   to demonstrate your skill in exploring, evaluating, and recording source material in a manner that shows how you have synthesized it

## Mapping out the area of exploration

Before you begin to explore the library, you must find a subject area that is appropriate for investigation. A good research topic will have the following characteristics:

**1.   Scope.** Your subject should be neither too broad nor too narrow in its focus.

*Example*

    *sleep — too broad*

    *why we sleep — not enough research material available*

    *what we now know about sleep and sleep disorders — more focussed*

2. **Support.** Your subject must be treated in written sources that are available to you. For example, a recent subject may not be a good choice because there may not yet be enough written about it. Also, remember that your sources must be treated objectively, so that the final paper reflects what is known about a subject, rather than just what you believe to be true about a subject. For example, your discussion of sleep must attempt to integrate the reader's questions about sleep with what advances the research has made.

3. **Significance.** Find something that you want to explore and that needs exploration. It would not, for instance, be enough to announce that you were going to show what new understanding scientists have reached in the study of brain chemicals affecting sleep. You must explain how these chemicals operate.

## Finding a working bibliography

Read widely at first to locate the best sources. Then read deeply in order to get at the heart of the matter. Explore the topic with your tentative thesis in mind, revising it as you go along.

1. Find general information in an encyclopedia, dictionary, or other reference book. Remember, though, that these general sources only scratch the surface.

2. Find information in the library computer system, microfiche, or card catalogue. Look under the subject heading or use the names of authors or titles that you have found in any of the encyclopedias you consulted.

    In the case at hand, to find information on sleep, look up SLEEP and related topics under the subject heading in the library card catalogue or on the computer.

3. Consult periodical indexes for further information. Often the periodical will give you more current material than is available in books. The Canadian Periodical Index (CPI) lists all articles published in Canadian journals for a given year.

4. As an alternative to looking through indexes and abstracts for information on a subject, you can have a search performed for you by computer. Most college and university libraries have an on-line search service.

    The advantages of a computer search are that it is quick, thorough, and up-to-date. In most college and university libraries, there is a charge for having this service performed. There are many factors that affect the cost of a search, such as the complexity of the search strategy, the cost of the database(s) searched, the number of references found and printed, and even the time of day. Nevertheless, most searches required by an undergraduate student should cost only $5 to $15. Your library's on-line searcher can usually give you an estimate before beginning the search.

The whole field of using computers to find information is changing very rapidly. The best way to know what is happening **RIGHT NOW** is to ask your reference librarian, who will bring you up-to-date on the technology and, more importantly, the choices available in your particular college or university library. If you have Netscape Navigator, you can perform your own searches at home.

5. Examine your sources with your specific topic in mind. Check the table of contents and the index of the books you find to search for suitable material.

6. Note down bibliographical information for any of the sources you consult. Small note cards $(3" \times 5")$ $(7.6 \times 12.7$ cm$)$ are useful. Record the library call numbers for your sources.

7. Follow the rules of documentation that apply to your discipline at this stage, and you will save time and trouble toward the end.

Although the sample research essay shown in this book is in the style of the American Psychological Association, some disciplines demand other styles of documentation. For example, English instructors often require that an essay's format follow the guidelines of the Modern Language Association, as shown in the sample literary essays on pp. 91 and 97. Ask your instructor if in doubt.

## Drawing up an outline

An outline for a research essay takes its direction from your preparatory reading. Follow the instructions in Chapter 4 on how to design an outline with these precautions in mind:

**SAMPLE BIBLIOGRAPHY CARD**

Gibaldi, Joseph.

MLA Handbook for Writers of Research

Papers. 4th. ed. New York: Modern

Language Association, 1995.

LB 2369. M57

1. Your outline must be flexible enough to accommodate all the information pertinent to your thesis statement.
2. Your outline must be fair and must reflect an objective approach to the material.
3. Your outline must be firmly established in your mind so that it does not attempt to include more material than can be adequately handled within the limits of the assignment.
4. Your outline is designed to be used. In the case of a research essay, the outline dictates the direction of your note-taking. It should help you stay on track in your explorations and help you limit yourself to what is possible.

## Recording source material

Like an explorer, you must accurately record the steps of your journey. You need a system. Here are some suggestions to simplify the task:

1. Take notes on large index cards (4" × 6" (10.2 × 15.2 cm) should do).
2. Identify the source on each card as briefly as possible. Usually, a last name and a page number will do.
3. Quote or paraphrase as the occasion demands (remember that too much quotation is dull). In addition, paraphrasing as you read will help you make sense of the material.
4. Limit yourself generally to one note per card to make sorting easier. This tactic will keep you from unconsciously relying too heavily on any one source.
5. Sort through your material at intervals to decide where it will fit into your working outline. If it won't fit, revise the outline or throw the irrelevant information out — no matter how attractive it is.
6. Copy accurately. If the passage is very lengthy, photocopy it to ensure precision, but be aware of copyright laws.

## Why bother?

Note-taking is such a painful chore that it is tempting not to do it. Don't succumb to the temptation. Note-taking is an essential part of research. It will help you determine the value of your sources. Ask these questions as you take notes:

1. Are the sources reliable?
2. Are they recent?
3. Are the sources themselves respected and well reviewed by others?
4. What are your own reactions to the sources?

This last point shows the need to record your own reactions to source material as you proceed. Add these ideas to your note cards to help you develop ideas later. You can differentiate them from source material by adding your initials.

Remember, the object of research is not to record facts, but to evaluate and synthesize your findings about an unsettled matter according to the viewpoint or thesis of your paper.

## Writing and documenting your essay

Prepare an outline, complete with intended patterns of argument, as suggested in Chapters 4 and 5 of this text. Then, write the first draft of your essay's introduction, body, and conclusion. This time, however, you must make sure to acknowledge your debt to any source as you write. One good way to do so is to include an abbreviated version of the source in parentheses immediately following the quoted matter in your essay.

### *Example*

> A survey done in the United States in 1977 showed sleep disorders to be especially troublesome for "blacks, women, poor people, the elderly, and those who were divorced, widowed, or separated" (Gaylin, 1977, p. 101).

This example not only shows the ease of abbreviation, but also demonstrates the ease of the APA style of documentation. It is also an example of the benefits of good preliminary note-taking.

For more information on documentation in MLA, APA, and traditional footnote style, see Chapter 14.

## Control

The special challenge of the research paper is to handle your source material in a controlled way. To control your research essay, remember these guidelines:

1. **Keep it limited.** Qualify the aim of your essay and stay within the limits of the thesis and the assignment.

2. **Keep it concise.** Avoid pretentious diction.
   (See Chapter 3 for more information.)

3. **Keep it formal.** This suggestion may even mean that you should not use the pronoun "I," in order to maintain objectivity (although it is often acceptable to do so). Ask your instructor for specific advice on this point.

4. **Keep it clean.** Small errors reduce the essay's credibility as an accurate record of research.

5. **Make it yours.** Don't lose yourself in assembled bits of research. Assimilate the material. Learn from it. What you include and how you use it determine your success as a researcher.

## ■ Sample Research Essay

The following is a sample research essay whose format conforms to the new APA guidelines. Study it carefully, noting the format and the method of documentation.

Number all
pages in the
top right corner
of the page.

Sleep: The Unconquered Realm

Carol Andrews

Health Sciences 100

Professor Griffin

Use abbreviated title as running head throughout essay.

Sleep: The Unconquered Realm

It is 4 a.m., and for the fourth consecutive night Matthew Schneider, business executive, has been lying in his bed counting sheep, trying frantically for five hours to fall asleep. Matthew, who has become grouchy and moody, has begun to fear that his loss of sleep will drastically affect his on-the-job performance.

Mary Smith, a first-year elementary school teacher, works hard all day with her thirty-two children, and in the evening she plays tennis and swims. Mary, however, never goes to bed until at least 2 a.m., always rising at 4 a.m. sharp. She feels healthy and happy, but lately friends have told her that her irreverence for a proper night's sleep is shortening her life and dulling her mind. No matter how hard she tries, though, after four hours of sleep — even on the weekends — Mary simply has to get out of bed.

Mr. and Mrs. Abe Kleitmann are the parents of a lively three-year-old daughter, Jessica, who will not sleep more than five hours at night. Repeatedly told that children must have a lot of sleep, the Kleitmanns are beginning to fear that Jessica is not normal.

These hypothetical cases, typical of those flowing into sleep clinics springing up across North America, are like experiences we all have had or like those we have heard others describe. Sleep, in short, affects us all. Most of us give up seven or eight hours a day — roughly a third of our lives — to sleep, and we think very little about it unless it becomes a problem. Sleep is, however, a major problem for many. Wilse Webb (1975b), one of the foremost sleep researchers, reports that about 14 percent of the population, or about one person in seven, suffers sleep disorders. A survey done in the United States in 1977 showed sleep disorders to be especially troublesome for "blacks, women, poor people, the elderly, and those who were divorced, widowed, or separated" (Gaylin, 1977, p. 101). Clearly, large portions of the population are troubled by sleep disorders, but available treatment is handicapped by the riddles of sleep research, a study that has flourished only in the last twenty years or so. Although

Use the abbreviation p. for "page" and pp. for "pages".

the sheer abundance of current information conveys the impression that

science is standing on the threshold of discoveries that affect millions of lives,

sleep research is still a giant maze of conflicting hypotheses and speculations.

Indeed, understanding sleep remains one of our most challenging frontiers.

 There are two central theories that attempt to explain why human

beings sleep: the adaptive theory and the restorative theory. The adaptive

theory claims that our need for sleep results from evolution. Webb (1975b)

theorizes that over millions of years each species evolved the sleep pattern that

best enabled it to survive. His hypothesis is simply that "sleep . . . evolved in

each species as a form of 'non-behavior' when not responding in the

environment would increase survival chances" (pp. 158-159). "Researchers

say that real sleep — measured by changes in electrical brain activity — occurs

only in warm-blooded animals with well-developed forebrains. But you can find

something that looks like sleep . . . in creatures as ancient and lowly as the

cockroach" (Rause, 1997). The differences between the sleep patterns of

various species do not seem to depend on physiological processes but reflect

the species' needs for safety. A lion, which does not fear many other animals,

may sleep soundly sixteen hours a day, but a gazelle, prey for many beasts, is a

short, light sleeper (Scarf, 1973, p. 86). Prehistoric humans would have found

it safer to sleep, particularly in the dark nights not lighted up with electric

bulbs and neon signs, than to prowl in harm's way.

Include author's name and date after each reference.

 The adaptive theory is interesting and convincing in many ways, but it

does not explain adequately why people today with their twenty-four-hour

lighting and sophisticated methods of obtaining food and fighting off predators

have not evolved a sleep pattern of one or two hours per night. If sleep is not

restorative but is simply an evolutionary result, why do modern human beings

need to sleep at all? Will our descendants, continuing the evolutionary process,

need less sleep than we? Hume (1983) claims that some of our sleep is obligatory

and allows for the restitution of the cerebrum, while the remainder is not really

essential, but just a method by which we occupy ourselves during darkness.

Ernest Hartmann (1973), on the other hand, believes that "sleep basically has a restorative function, in accordance with our own commonsense notions" (p. 145). He believes that sleep consolidates disruptive, stressful events of the day into a person's normal emotional and learning systems, especially since it is clear that most people do require more sleep and dream-sleep after stressful experiences or strenuous learning experiences. Although tests with sleep deprivation bear out some of Hartmann's theories, the hypothesis that sleep is basically restorative is problematic because, as Webb (1975b) states, "'what' is being diminished and, in turn, 'restored' has been so elusive that is has not been specifiable" (pp. 162-163). The only clear observation is that the reasons we sleep are enormously complex.

Include page references only with direct quotations.

A good deal of sleep research has been concerned with pinpointing the amount of sleep a person needs. Although most young adults seem to need, or believe that they need, six to eight hours of sleep per night, scientists have found a great variation in the quantity of sleep required by adults. For example, a husband worried about his wife's habitual four-hour-per-night sleeping pattern took her to a sleep clinic, where doctors found her sleep "remarkably efficient" and pronounced her very healthy. Doctors at the same clinic examined a physics professor about fifty years old who was concerned because he believed he needed to sleep at least fourteen hours a night. They found that he was absolutely correct in his assessment: he slept in normal patterns that stretched out over fourteen hours. Cutting his sleep by even two hours left him tired (Scarf, 1973). And, although older people generally do not require as much sleep as young adults, some astounding cases have been found of old people who hardly sleep at all, for example, a seventy-year-old physically sound woman who sleeps only one hour per night (Webb, 1975a).

The story is also told — though it has not been scientifically certified — of the artist Salvador Dali's famous method of sleep. Dali reportedly sat in a chair, holding a spoon over a tin plate that he had situated behind the chair. He relaxed. As he fell asleep, the spoon dropped from his hand, banging against the tin plate and waking him. He said that the sleep he got in the very tiny interval that passed between the time the spoon fell and the time it struck the tin was enough for him (Dement, 1974).

How much sleep is normal? The amount of time a human being needs to sleep may well be hereditary, although such factors as prenatal care, illness, nutrition, and environment play a role in determining the necessary quantity of sleep (Webb, 1975b). Even though most people seem to require about the same amount of sleep (something close to the proverbial eight hours), scientists agree that each person's requirement for sleep is individual. What they do not agree on is whether great variations in the quantity of sleep reflect basic differences in personality and intelligence.

On the basis of two studies in his laboratories, Webb (1975a) believes that sleep length shows "no more difference in people than big or little ears," that is, shows no basic difference in intelligence or personality or physical well-being (p. 31). Dr. Hartmann maintains, however, that there are basic differences between short and long sleepers. Those who need more sleep tend to be more neurotic and depressed and under greater stress than the shorter sleepers, who seem more vivacious, self-confident, and aggressive. The longer sleepers, though worriers, tend to be more creative, less conventional thinkers than short sleepers. However, Hartmann (1973) admits that it is not clear whether the sleep pattern produces the personality or whether the personality requires the particular sleep pattern. He is convinced only that there is a correlation between the quantity of sleep and certain traits.

How we sleep — that is, the individual phases that make up a night's sleep — is one of the few non-controversial areas of sleep research, but scientists do not know exactly why or how a person falls asleep. Even the electroencephalogram (EEG), which is used to chart the brain waves that reveal sleep patterns, cannot show the precise instant when sleep begins (Dement, 1974). Once it has begun, however, normal sleep is made up of five distinct stages, which recur during the night in cycles of about ninety minutes.

The normal sleeper passes fairly quickly through Stage-1 and Stage-2 sleep (light sleep phases differing in the kinds of brain waves) into the transitional Stage-3 sleep and into the intense, deep sleep of Stage 4. From Stage 4, or Deep Sleep as it is often called, the sleeper passes again through Stage-1, Stage-2, and Stage-3 sleep into Stage 4, rarely skipping a stage but changing stages about thirty-five times (Webb, 1975b). After he or she has passed through the sleep stages once, however, this sequence is interrupted regularly — often at the end of Stage 2 — by a separate and very puzzling stage called Rapid Eye Movement sleep, or REM sleep, so called because it is characterized by bursts of eye movement along with brain waves somewhat like those of Stage-1 sleep. Until this REM sleep was first observed in 1952 by Nathaniel Kleitman and Eugene Asperinsky, sleep was thought to be a process from waking to intense, deep sleep and back to waking. Now, however, it is obvious that sleep is cyclic (Hartmann, 1973). Most people follow this basic sequence of stages, but no two people sleep in exactly the same pattern.

The discovery of REM sleep revolutionized sleep research. Studying the correlation of REM sleep and dreaming has led to numerous hypotheses about the significance and function of both REM sleep and dreaming. Many of the theories that attempt to explain the function of REM sleep claim that it is a necessary tool for the consolidation of new material into long-term memory. Dr. Peter Hauri, director of the Dartmouth Sleep Laboratory at Hanover, New Hampshire, and Boston researchers Chester Pearlman and Ramon Greenberg are among the scientists who claim that REM sleep not only aids memory, but also allows the individual to absorb the stressful experiences suffered during the day (Scarf, 1973).

On the other hand, others find that REM sleep does not seem to aid memory at all. Webb (1975b) finds that extreme deprivation of REM sleep has little effect on the individual. Dement, whose first (and now largely disproved) theory about REM sleep was that it was a psychological stabilizer the loss of which caused emotional disturbances (Scarf, 1973), has recently speculated that "perhaps REM sleep is necessary for the normal pre- and post-natal maturation of the brain" and its real function is served long before we become adults (Dement, 1974, p. 31). In short, the precise function of REM — like so many other questions about sleep — continues to baffle researchers.

One particularly interesting recent discovery with regard to sleep and memory is the Prior-Sleep Effect, a phenomenon that suggests that certain sleep is detrimental to the memory. The Prior-Sleep Effect has shown that up to four hours of sleep just before learning has a detrimental effect on long-term memory. Even as little as one half-hour of sleep just before hitting the books is harmful to a student's memory. If the student sleeps as much as six hours before attempting to study, he or she will be more successful at remembering. Bruce Ekstrand and his co-workers (1977), although convinced that "sleep facilitates memory" (p. 419), have found that "four hours sleep prior to learning resulted in more forgetting than no sleep prior to learning" (p. 431). The Prior-Sleep Effect does not, however, affect short-term memory. Thus a student may be able to learn enough information after three hours' sleep to pass a midterm test, but when final exams roll around in a couple of months, he or she will have to rememorize the information.

Ekstrand and his team speculate that the Prior-Sleep Effect is caused by the gradual buildup in the brain of a chemical that blocks the integration of information from the short-term memory into the long-term memory. They believe that the chemical subsides when a person wakes, gradually diminishing to allow the memory to function. This chemical, a hormone called somatotrophin, has recently been found to increase in the sleeper's body, beginning within a half-hour after he or she falls asleep. Though the hormone level diminishes toward the end of the night, it is high during the first four hours of sleep (Hoddes, 1977).

Somatotrophin, which may account for the Prior-Sleep Effect, is not the only body chemical that plays an important role in sleep. The neurochemical serotonin is now believed to be somewhat responsible both for the onset of sleep and for Stage-4 sleep, and the chemical norepinephrine may help to bring about REM sleep. Sleeping pills of all kinds, though they do produce some phases of sleep, interfere with these chemicals and other brain chemistry, upsetting regular sleep stages (Scarf, 1973). There is, however, a natural sedative built into certain foods, a sedative that is compatible with the neurochemicals. This sedative, tryptophan, is found in milk, eggs, and meat. Its presence accounts for the sleepiness we often feel after a big meal or after the glass of warm milk that we may drink to help us sleep (Scarf, 1973).

But what happens to a person who is deprived of all sleep or deprived of all REM sleep or all Stage-4 sleep? Experimenters have found some surprising data about the effects of sleep deprivation.

Early sleep researchers doubtless believed that the loss of sleep was physically harmful because, in the first sleep deprivation experiment conducted in 1894 by Marie de Manaceine, puppies deprived of all sleep died after four to six days (Dement, 1974). Not only do human beings not die when deprived of sleep, but the physiological changes in a sleep-deprived person are few and fairly insignificant, though after five days of sleep loss, emotional changes are noted (Webb, 1975b). A sleep-deprived person can do well at almost any brief laboratory test, although motivation is a crucial problem, and performance on more complicated tasks may be impaired.

> . . . the general conclusion about performance seems to be that highly motivated subjects can perform almost any task that requires a short-term effort. On the other hand, sustained periods of performance will typically show deterioration, particularly if they are routine or "dull." Two major exceptions seem to be tasks that require rapid and complex reaction time and short-term memory tasks. These latter involve such things as listening to a series of digits and immediately recalling them. (Webb, 1975b, pp. 126-127)

Indent long quotations five spaces.

If we are reasonably efficient when we do not sleep and if our bodies do not suffer serious harm when deprived of sleep, why then do we feel sleepy?

Why do we waste a third of our lives sleeping? Dement (1974) believes that the time a person spends in sleep is "the depressed phases of his circadian rhythm," that is, the cyclic, rhythmic movement that permeates all things — the planets, the tides, the seasons, and all of life (pp. 18-19). This theory may account for the poorer performance of sleep-deprived persons who carry out tasks during periods when they normally would sleep. Webb (1975b) observes that outside the laboratory, this decreased efficiency during the individual's normal sleeping time is evidenced in industry's need to provide more intensive quality control and more safety checks for those workers who rotate to the odd-hour shifts.

Understanding how we sleep and why is obviously an enormously complex challenge that cuts across physiological, psychological, and biochemical research. Scientists are turning up more and more questions about the extent to which sleep affects everyone. Can sleep deprivation be used to treat mental disorders? (Bhanji, 1977). To what degree are physical illnesses responsible for sleep disorders, and vice versa? Do sleep problems cause mental disorders? In 1961, after a British case in which an American soldier was acquitted of the murder of his girlfriend on the grounds that he was asleep when he killed her, the House of Lords debated whether the verdict in such cases should henceforth be "guilty, but asleep" (Casady, 1976, p. 83).

To most of humanity, sleep seems a simple thing. In 335 B.C., Aristotle wrote: "When they are asleep you cannot tell a poor man from a bad one, whence the saying that for half their lives there is no difference between the happy and the miserable" (quoted in "Sleep and dreams," 1974, p. 6). On the one hand, sleep is the great equalizer of humankind, a common denominator in a world of expanding diversity and complexity. On the other hand, however, even though sleep universally demands our time and respect, we are only beginning to understand — in a way that Aristotle did not — that sleep exacts its due with incredible variety and intricacy among people, a variety and intricacy that make sleep one of the great puzzles of science.

References

Bhanji, S. (1977). Treatment of depression by sleep deprivation. Nursing
    Times, 73, 540-541.

Casady, M. (1976, January). The sleepy murders. Psychology Today, 81, pp. 79, 83.

Dement, W. C. (1974). Some people must watch while some must sleep. San
    Francisco: Freeman.

Ekstrand, B. R. (1977). The effects of sleep on human long-term memory. In
    R. R. Drucker-Cohen & J. L. McGaugh (Eds.), Neurobiology of sleep and
    memory (pp. 239-252). New York: Academic Press.

Gaylin, J. (1977, April). Sleep: Tracking the elusive sandman. Social Science
    and Medicine, 10; Psychology Today 96, p. 101.

Hartmann, E. L. (1973). The functions of sleep. New Haven: Yale University Press.

Hoddes, E. (1977, June). Does sleep help you study? Psychology Today, 98, p. 69.

Hume, K. I. (1983). The rhythmical nature of sleep. In A. Mayes (Ed.), Sleep
    mechanisms and functions in human animals: An evolutionary perspective
    (pp. 18-57). Wokingham, Berkshire, UK: Van Nostrand Reinhold.

Nature's sleeping pill (1973, October 13). Newsweek, 114, 69.

Scarf, M. (1973, October 21). Oh for a decent night's sleep! The New York
    Times Magazine, 117, 67, 70, 72, 77-78, 81, 84, 86.

Sleep and dreams: Where are you when the lights go out? (1974, December).
    Harper's, 96, 5-12, 109-113.

Sleep for the memory. (1976, August 23). Time, 65, 39.

Rause, V. (1997, January 9 ). One man's quest for a good night's sleep.
    Discovery Online [On-line]. Available: Netscape. World Wide Web.
    http://www.discovery.com/area/specials/sleep/sleep1.html

Webb, W. B. (1975a, August 22). On sleep: The long and the short of it. The
    New York Times, p. 31.

Webb, W. B. (1975b). Sleep: The gentle tyrant. Englewood Cliffs, NJ:
    Prentice-Hall.

Webb, W. B., & Agnew, Jr., H. W. (1973). Sleep and dreams. Dubuque, IA: Brown.

Note differences between capitalization of book and periodicals.

Indent references three spaces except for the first line.

Note the authors' first names are reduced to initials.

When you use two works by one author that appear in the same year, differentiate them by using a, b, and so on.

# PART FIVE

# Documenting and Delivering Your Paper

# Planning Your Paper's Layout

When you organize your final printed manuscript for submission to an instructor, you need to be careful to meet the specifications demanded for the paper's presentation. The paper should be easy to read, neat, and presented in a style consistent with a standard form of documentation. The specifications you follow depend, in large part, on whether you are using the MLA, APA, or University of Chicago style of documentation. Each of these styles requires certain things of the manuscript. For the sake of consistency, follow these guidelines as closely as you can.

## ◼ The Layout of a Paper in MLA Style

You will likely follow these guidelines if you study English or Philosophy, Classics, or Visual Arts.

1. Use letter-quality medium-weight paper, $8\frac{1}{2}$" × 11" (22 × 28 cm).
2. Make sure the print quality is sharp, and the font is commonly accepted. Do not use decorative fonts. Use either italics or underlining consistently throughout.
3. Double-space everything.
4. Leave one-inch (2.54-cm) margins. Do not justify the right margin. Indent paragraphs five spaces. Indent long quotations ten spaces from the left with a normal right margin.
5. Place page numbers in the upper right-hand corner beside your last name (without a page abbreviation or a comma).
6. On the first page, place your name, the course name, your instructor's name, and the date in the upper left corner. Two lines below, centre the paper's title, without underlining, italicizing, or quotation marks.
7. Use a paper clip to attach the pages.
8. Keep a copy for your own protection.
9. Refer to the sample MLA essays on pp. 91 and 97.

## ◼ The Layout of a Paper in APA Style

When you use APA style for a manuscript, you are probably preparing a paper in the Social Sciences, where the date of publication is particularly important. Follow these guidelines for the proper preparation of a paper in APA style:

1. Use heavy-weight white bond paper, $8\frac{1}{2}" \times 11"$ ($22 \times 28$ cm).
2. Use a clear font or typeface. Times Roman and Courier are preferred. Use underlining within your manuscript.
3. Double-space everything. Triple- or quadruple-space between elements of your paper.
4. Use one-inch (2.54-cm) margins. Indent paragraphs five spaces. Indent long quotations ten spaces.
5. Use a shortened version of the paper's title as a header in the upper right-hand corner of each page. Number pages without an abbreviation for page or any punctuation.
6. Make a separate title page. The top line will be the header and the page number. At the left margin, type the words "Running Head:" and a shortened version of the title. Centre the title and capitalize major words. Include other identifying information, centred, and then centre the page vertically.
7. Use headings to separate sections of the paper, if desired. Centre main headings, all in capitals; type the next level of headings flush left, with ordinary capitalization; indent the next level of headings with only the first word capitalized, and follow these headings with a period, with the text continuing after one space.
8. Use a paper clip to attach the pages.
9. Keep a copy for your own protection.
10. Refer to the sample APA essay on pp. 111–120.

## ■ The Layout of a Paper in University of Chicago Style

The University of Chicago Style is often used in disciplines like History, where notes are extremely important. There are some major differences between the look of a manuscript in MLA or APA and University of Chicago style. The following list should make the changes clear:

1. Use heavy-weight white bond paper, $8\frac{1}{2}" \times 11"$ ($22 \times 28$ cm).
2. Use a clear, standard font, like Times Roman and Courier in pica (12-point size) or elite (10-point size). Letter-quality print is preferred. Use either italics or underlining for titles.
3. Double-space most of the paper. Footnotes, endnotes, indented quotations, and visual elements are single-spaced, though separated by double-spacing.
4. Use a one-and-one-half-inch (3.8-cm) margin on the left. On the first page, the top margin must be two inches (5 cm); subsequent pages must be one inch (2.54 cm).
5. Number pages either at the top right corner or at the top centre of each page. The first page of a section has a page number at the bottom, centred.
6. Make a separate title page, centred vertically and horizontally. Do not count the title page in your numbering.
7. Centre the title of your paper two inches (5 cm) from the top of the next page. Leave three spaces and begin the text.

8. If you use headings, make sure the first-level headings are centred, underlined, with important words capitalized; the next level should be centred and with ordinary capitalization, but not underlined; the next level should begin at the left margin, underlined and with ordinary capitalization.
9. Use a paper clip to attach pages.
10. Keep a copy for your own protection.

# Documenting — MLA, APA, and University of Chicago Guidelines

> Whatever has been well said by anyone is mine.
> *Seneca*

**Y**our bibliography should list all items that you quote, paraphrase, or use as source material. Three basic styles of documentation will be covered in this section: MLA style, most commonly used in the humanities; APA style, often used in the social sciences; and University of Chicago style, often used in history and other disciplines that prefer a traditional footnotes (or endnote) style.

## ■ Sample Bibliographical Entries in MLA Style

The examples that follow show how certain entries would appear in a bibliography, if you follow the guidelines of the Modern Language Association. These entries should serve as models when you prepare your own bibliography page. In MLA style, this page is called "Works Cited." If you need further information, consult Joseph Gibaldi, *MLA Handbook for Writers of Research Papers.* 4th ed. (New York: Modern Language Association, 1995).

### Books
**One author:**
Frazer, James George. The Golden Bough: A Study in Magic and
    Religion. New York: Macmillan, 1922.

Use a shortened version of the publisher's name (in this case, Macmillan Publishing Company), making sure that your label for the company is still recognizable. Include complete subtitles in bibliographical entries, and underline title and subtitle continuously.

**Two authors and edition (if not the first edition):**
Strunk, William, Jr., and E. B. White. The Elements of Style. 3rd ed.
    New York: Macmillan, 1979.

**Three authors:**
Bercuson, David, J. L. Granatstein, and W. R. Young. Sacred Trust?
    Brian Mulroney and the Conservative Party in Power. Toronto:
    Doubleday, 1986.

**More than three authors:**
Cornell, Paul G., et al. Canada: Unity in Diversity. Toronto: Holt,
    1967.

**Corporate author:**
Imperial Oil Limited. The Review. Toronto: Imperial Oil, Spring 1987.

**Editor:**
Drabble, Margaret, ed. The Oxford Companion to English Literature.
    5th ed. Oxford: Oxford UP, 1985.

**Government publication:**
Canada. Minister of Supply and Services Canada. Canada Year Book
    1985. Ottawa: Statistics Canada, 1985.

**Story or article from an anthology:**
Cohen, Dian. "Trading Commodities." Prose Models. Ed. Gerald
    Levin, David Hampton, and Gerald Lynch. 3rd Canadian ed.
    Toronto: Harcourt Brace, 1997. 210-13.

**Translation:**
Ringuet. Thirty Acres. Trans. Felix and Dorothea Walker. Toronto:
    McClelland and Stewart, 1960.

**Reprint:**
Montgomery, L. M. Anne of Green Gables. 1908. Toronto:
    McGraw-Hill, 1968.

The original hardcover edition was published in 1908. The paperback version
appeared in 1968.

**A work in more than one volume:**
Rollins, Hyder Edward, ed. The Letters of John Keats: 1814-1821. 2
    vols. Cambridge: Harvard UP, 1958.

**A work in a series:**
Woodman, Ross. James Reaney. Canadian Writers New Canadian
    Library 12. Toronto: McClelland and Stewart, 1971.

The volume number is given in Arabic numerals and without the abbreviation
*vol.*

## Magazines, newspapers, and journals
**Unsigned article:**
"Deal on West Bank, Hebron in Final Stages." The Globe and Mail 14
    Jan. 1997, natl. ed.: A10.

The names of months other than May, June, and July are usually abbreviated. "A10" refers to the section and page number of the newspaper.

**Daily newspapers:**
Renzetti, Elizabeth. "Much Ado About Opera." The Globe and Mail 18
    Jan. 1997, natl. ed.: C8.

When not part of the newspaper's name, the city's name should be given in brackets after the title.

**Weekly magazine or newspaper:**
Steacy, Anne, and Ben Barber. "Losing the Race Against Drug
    Dealers." Maclean's 18 Aug. 1986: 46.

**Monthly or bi-monthly magazine:**
Brown, Andrew. "The Freedom Portfolio." Your Money May-June
    1986: 61-62.

**Journal — continuous pagination through the year:**
Campbell, Jane. " 'Competing Towers of Babel': Some Patterns of
    Language in Hard Times." English Studies in Canada 10.4
    (1984), 416-35.

When the pages of a journal are numbered consecutively through the year, a comma precedes the page reference. Note also that an issue number ("4" in this case) follows the volume number "10." They are separated by a period.

**Journal — separate pagination for each issue:**
Davis, Marie. "Parable, Parody, or 'Blip in the Canadian Literary
    Landscape': Tom King on A Coyote Christmas Story." Canadian
    Children's Literature 84 (1996): 24-36.

When the pages of a journal are numbered separately for each issue, a colon precedes the page reference.

**Editorial:**
"Considering Refugees." Editorial. The Globe and Mail 7 May 1987: A6.

**Book review:**
Miller, J. R. Rev. of The Man from Halifax: Sir John Thompson,
    Prime Minister, by P. B. Waite. Queen's Quarterly 93 (1986):
    646-48.


## Encyclopedia
**Signed with name or initials:**
So[utham], B[rian] C. "Austen, Jane." Encyclopaedia Britannica:
    Macropaedia. 1974 ed.

This article appears with the initials "B.C. So." appended to it. To identify it, you need only check the index of the encyclopedia and enclose the added information in brackets.

## Unsigned article:
"Literature." The Cambridge Encyclopedia. 1994 ed.

## Government publication:
Canada. Royal Commission on Aboriginal Peoples. Public Policy and
    Aboriginal People 1985-1992 Volume 2. Restructuring the
    Relationship. Ottawa: Ministry of Supply and Services, Canada,
    1996.

Canada. House of Commons. Standing Committee on Aboriginal
    Affairs. Minutes of Proceedings and Evidence of the Standing
    Committee on Aboriginal Affairs. 19 March 1990, Issue No. 22.
    Ottawa: Queen's Printer, 1990. 14-15.

The government agency is considered the author, unless the name of the author
is given.

## Pamphlets, bulletins, and reports
Canada. Veterans Affairs Canada. A Day of Remembrance. Ottawa:
    Government of Canada, 1984.

## Unpublished dissertations
DuBroy, Michael Thomas. "The Tale of the Folk: Revolution and the
    Late Prose Romances of William Morris." Diss. U of Western
    Ontario, 1982.

## Micropublications
Books or periodicals in microprint form are documented as they would be in their
original form.

## Non-print sources

### Motion picture:
My Financial Career. National Film Board. 1962.

### Television or radio program:
"The Gender Tango." Women: A True Story. CTV. CKCO-TV,
    Kitchener, ON. 20 Jan. 1997.

### Television interview:
Mirren, Helen. Interview by Brian Linehan. Linehan. CHCH,
    Hamilton. 18 Jan. 1997.

### Film:
Everybody Says I Love You. Dir. Woody Allen. Miramax, 1997.

### Video:
It's a Wonderful Life. Dir. Frank Capra. 1946. Videocassette.
    Republic, 1993.

Include the title, director, distributor, and year. Note that the original year is included before the distribution information. Include other information such as writer or performers, if relevant.

**Performance of stage play:**
Long Day's Journey into Night. By Eugene O'Neill. Dir. Diana
LeBlanc. Perf. Martha Henry,.William Hutt. Tom Patterson
Theatre, Stratford, 4 June 1995.

**Recording:**
Morissette, Alanis. Jagged Little Pill. Warner, 1995.

**Song:**
Morissette, Alanis. "Ironic." Jagged Little Pill. Warner, 1995.

## Electronic publications
**Electronic mail:**
Rockwell, Geoffrey. E-mail to the author. 11 Mar. 1997.

**A CD-ROM source:**
The Oxford English Dictionary. 2nd ed. CD-ROM. Oxford: Oxford UP,
1992.

*Use the same order of information for a CD-ROM from a previously published source, if the information is given:*

Last name of author, first name of author. Title. Place of print
publication: Publisher, Date. CD-ROM. City of CD-ROM
production: Producer, Electronic publication date. Access
number is optional.

**An On-line database with a printed analogue:**
Taylor, Ella. "The Thief, the Nurse, the Patient, and the Lover." A
Review of The English Patient. Atlantic Monthly Jan. 1997:
41-42. On-line. Netscape. World Wide Web. 20 Jan. 1997.
Available: http://www.theAtlantic.com/Atlantic/ae/97jan/
97janflm.htm#one. (Note: Use a closing period.)

*Use the same order of information as for a printed source, but add the word "On-line," provide the name of the computer service, and list the date on which you accessed the material. The path is optional, but might be required by the instructor.*

**Lecture:**
Gedalof, Allan. "Mystery Writing." U.W.O. Senior Alumni Series.
Wesanne McKellar Room, U of Western Ontario, London,
Ontario. 14 Apr. 1987.

**Interview:**
Wiseman, Adele. Personal Interview. 15 Apr. 1987.

For examples of citations of other non-print sources — games, globes, filmstrips, microscope slides, and transparencies — consult Eugene B. Fleischer's *A Style*

*Manual for Citing Microform and Nonprint Media* (Chicago: American Library Association, 1978).

# ■ Citing Sources in MLA Style

Whenever you refer to material from another source, whether book, journal article, motion picture, or recording, you must acknowledge your source. Citing your sources no longer necessitates footnotes or endnotes. Instead, citations of sources are placed in the body of the essay in parentheses. A footnote or endnote is necessary only if you have supplementary material to add that does not properly belong in the text of the essay itself.

## Simple citation

Include in parentheses after the citation only what is essential to guide the reader to the correct entry in the list of "Works Cited." Often, all that will be needed is the last name of the author followed by a page number. For example, if you were quoting from Margaret Laurence's *The Diviners*, the citation in the text would look like this:

> *Morag's collection of photographs gives the reader insight into her own hidden past. As she says, "I keep the snapshots not for what they show but for what is hidden in them" (Laurence 6).*

This citation refers the reader to the following entry on the "Works Cited" page:

> *Laurence, Margaret.* The Diviners. *Toronto: Bantam, 1974.*

If this is the only entry listed under Laurence, there is no confusion, and the reader knows that the quotation can be found on page 6 of the listed text.

## Citation of more than one work by the same author

If, on the other hand, there are references to two works by the same author, a more specific notation is required. Say that you referred in the same essay to Margaret Laurence's earlier novel, *A Jest of God*. You might, perhaps, make the following reference:

> *Rachel discovers her own capacity to hide the truth from herself. As she explains, "There is room enough in anyone's bonehouse for too much duplicity" (Laurence Jest 182).*

This reference makes it clear that more than one book by Laurence is listed in "Works Cited."

## Citation of a work in more than one volume

If, in an essay about Keats's poetry, you decide to quote from the two-volume collection of Keats's letters, the citation would read as follows:

> *Keats, in the composition of the odes, dedicates himself to the search for "the true voice of feeling" (Letters 2:167).*

Here the Arabic numeral 2 refers to the second volume of the letters. A colon is used to separate the volume number from the page number.

Similar adjustments must be made to clarify abbreviated citations. Always remember to ask yourself what the reader needs to know in order to find the reference easily.

### Citation of poetry and of long or short quotations

Avoid redundant citations. If the body of your essay already explains the source adequately, do not restate the information in parentheses. For example, you might write the following analysis of Keats's poetry:

> *The poet speaks of the lure of death in "Ode to a Nightingale":*
>
> *Darkling I listen; and, for many a time*
>     *I have been half in love with easeful Death,*
> *Call'd him soft names in many a mused rhyme,*
>     *To take into the air my quiet breath. (51-54)*

Here only the line numbers are listed in parentheses, since the title of the poem is given in the body of the essay itself. Note, too, that a long quotation is double-spaced, indented, and written without quotation marks. Because the quoted matter is poetry, the lines are given as they are in the text. If the quotation were only two lines long, it would be written in the body of the essay in the following way, using quotation marks:

> *The poet speaks of the lure of death in "Ode to a Nightingale": "Darkling I listen; and, for many a time/I have been half in love with easeful Death" (51-52).*

### Citation of poetic drama

A reference to a play must refer to act, scene, and line numbers, as in the following case:

> *In Shakespeare's* A Midsummer Night's Dream, *Titania, enchanted with Bottom, sees the world around with romantic eyes. As she says,*
>
>     *The moon methinks looks with a watery eye;*
>     *And when she weeps, weeps every little flower,*
>     *Lamenting some enforced chastity. (3.1.202-04)*

### Punctuation of citations

Note that for citations within the text, punctuation appears *after* the parentheses. In quotations set off from the text, citations *follow* the final punctuation. To make citations as unobtrusive as possible, try to place them at the end, rather than in the middle, of sentences.

## ■ Sample Bibliographic Entries in APA Style

The following entries are arranged according to the style of the *Publication Manual of the American Psychological Association*. In this case, the bibliography is given the heading References. The APA uses an author–date system of citation. Here are some guidelines to citations in the reference pages. See also the References page of the APA model essay on p. 120 and consult this text:

American Psychological Association. (1994). Publication Manual of the American Psychological Association. 4th ed. Washington: Psychological Association.

## Information Needed for APA References

1. List alphabetically by last name. Use initials instead of first or middle names.
2. Include the year next in parentheses. Include the month or day if given.
3. List complete titles and subtitles.
4. Include these items in the following order: translator, edition number, volume number, issue number if the journal is paginated by issue, and inclusive pages.
5. Take publication information from books in this way: use an abbreviated form of the publisher's name, the first city listed, and the most recent date. From periodicals, get this information: the volume number, issue number (if relevant), and date.

## APA Format in References

1. For "unpolished" manuscripts, indent the first line five to seven spaces (the default setting on your word processor is acceptable). For finished manuscripts, "hanging indents" are used, as illustrated in the following examples. The latter format is recommended. However, the APA guidelines defer to your professor's style preference, so you should clarify this before submitting your paper.
2. List authors by last names and initials. If a work is co-authored, invert the names of all the authors and use an ampersand (&) to join the final name.
3. For books, capitalize the first word of the title and of the subtitle as well as proper nouns and proper adjectives; everything else is lower case. For periodicals, use both upper and lower case as usual, a comma, and a volume number. Underline titles. Underline both title and volume number with a continuous underline.
4. Abbreviate names of commercial publishers by using only the main elements of the name. Cite names of university publishers in full.
5. Separate sections of entries with periods, even the words in parentheses. But separate the place of publication from the publisher's name by a colon and one space.
6. Use only one space between items in APA citations.
7. For articles, list the complete page range (211-214) and introduce it with the abbreviation pp. (for pages) or p. (for page).
8. The examples shown below are single-spaced to save paper. When you submit your paper, all entries should be double-spaced.

## Books

**One author:**
Selye, H. (1956). The stress of life. New York: McGraw-Hill.

**Two authors:**
Gatchel, R., & Baum, A. (1983). An introduction to health psychology. Reading, MA: Addison-Wesley.

## Journals

**One author:**

Turner, J. (1981). Social support as a contingency in psychological well-being. Journal of Health and Social Behavior, 22, 357-367.

**Multiple authors in a journal with separate paging:**

Blanton, S., Robin, B., & Kinzie, M. (1991). Repurposing a feature film for interactive multimedia. Educational Technology, 31(12), 7-12.

**Newspaper article:**

Gadd, Jane. (1997, January 14). Tax credit to target child poverty. The Globe and Mail, National Edition, p. A1.

**A review:**

Turbide, D. (1997, January 20). All about Eve [Review of the TV series Women: a true story]. Maclean's, 64.

**A film:**

Apted, M. (Director). (1994). Nell. [Film]. Beverly Hills: 20th Century-Fox.

## Electronic publications

**A CD-ROM source:**

On the brink: An interview with Yitzhak Rabin. (1994, April 23). [CD-ROM]. Jerusalem Post, 16. Available: Silverplatter: PAIS [Public Affairs Information Service] International item: 94-0504485 (Note: do not use a closing period after an item number.)

*Use the following form for a CD-ROM, generally:*

Author, I. (date). Title of article [CD-ROM]. Title of Journal, xx, xxx-xxx. Abstract from: Source and retrieval number

**An On-line journal article:**

Okrent, M. (1996). Why the mind isn't a program: (But some digital computer might have a mind). The Electronic Journal of Analytical Philosophy [On-line], 4. Available: http://www.phil. indiana.edu/ejap/ejap.html (Note: do not use a period after a path name.)

*Use the following form for an on-line journal, generally:*

Author, I. (date). Title of article. Name of periodical [On-line], xx. Available: Specify path

## ■ Citing Sources in APA Style

As with the MLA style of documentation, you may cite your sources in parentheses in APA style. In APA style, however, the year of publication is given with the author's last name; hence, the title of a work is not usually needed. Note details in the following examples:

**Short Quotation:**

*Social support is defined as "those relationships among people that provide not only material help and emotional assurance, but also the sense that one is a continuing object of concern on the part of other people" (Pilsuk, 1982, p. 20).*

**Long Quotation:**

*Seligman (1975) argues that helplessness may lead to depression:*

*Those people who are particularly susceptible to depression may have had lives relatively devoid of mastery; their lives may have been full of situations in which they were helpless to influence the sources of suffering and relief. (p. 104)*

Note that, in this passage, the author's last name and the date of publication are not included in parentheses because they are already given in the body of the essay.

**Paraphrase:**

*Cobb (1976) insists that stress, not social support, is the key to understanding changes in health. Social support only acts as a buffer.*

Following these basic guidelines should help you assemble your notes and your bibliography with relative ease. Remember these guidelines as you prepare the documentation for your essay:

1. Be consistent.
2. Give your reader all the information needed to find a reference.
3. Check the sample research essay in this guide for a model of APA format.
4. Check the appropriate style guide for further details.

# ■ Sample Bibliographic Entries in University of Chicago Style

Some disciplines, in particular history and political science, prefer a traditional footnoting style. The best source of information about this style are Kate Turabian's *A Manual for Writers* and *The Chicago Manual of Style*.

If your instructor advises you to use this traditional style, rather than the parenthetical forms just outlined, refer to this section.

Since bibliographic listings can be complex, try to include as much information as possible in each entry. Remember that you are trying to help your reader locate the sources.

## Books
**One author:**
Miller, J. S. Skyscrapers Hide the Heavens: A History of Indian-White Relations in Canada. Toronto: University of Toronto Press, 1989.

**Two authors and component part in a larger work:**
Rogers, E. S., and Flora Tobobondung. "Parry Sound Farmers: A Period of Change in the Way of Life of the Algonkians of Southern Ontario." In Contributions to Canadian Ethnology, edited by David Brez Carlisle. Ottawa: National Museums of Canada, 1975.

**More than three authors:**
Martin, Nancy, Pat D'Arcy, Bryan Newton, and Robert Parker. Writing and Learning Across the Curriculum 11-16. Upper Montclair, N.J.: Boynton/Cook, 1976.

Note that it would be permissible to shorten the note form of this entry to read:

[1] Nancy Martin and others, Writing and Learning Across the Curriculum 11-16 (Upper Montclair, N.J.: Boynton/Cook, 1976), 50.

**Edition after the first:**
Barker, Larry L. Communication. 4th ed. Englewood Cliffs, N.J.: Prentice-Hall, 1987.

**Association author and reprint:**
Nin.Da.Waab.Jig. Minishenhying Anishnaabe-aki Walpole Island: The Soul of Indian Territory. Windsor: Commercial Associates/Ross Roy Ltd., 1987; reprint, 1989.

This book is by a Native community, and the title is in Ojibwa. The name of the community is listed first.

It is important to list information about a reprint, in case changes have been made to the pagination.

**Editor:**
Storr, Anthony, ed. The Essential Jung. Selected and Introduced by Anthony Storr. Princeton, N.J.: Princeton University Press, 1983.

**Translation:**
Pushkin, Alexander. Eugene Onegin. Trans. by Charles Johnston with an Introduction by John Bayley. Harmondsworth, Middlesex: Penguin, 1977.

**A work in more than one volume:**
Campbell, Joseph. The Masks of God. 4 vols. New York: Viking Press, 1960-68.

**A work in a series:**
Stanley, George F. G. The War of 1812: Land Operations. Canadian War Museum Historical Publication, no. 18. Toronto: Macmillan, 1983.

**Component part by one author in a work by another:**
Purvis, Jane. "The Experience of Schooling for Working-Class Boys and Girls in Nineteenth Century England." In Defining the Curriculum: Histories and Ethnographies, edited by Ivor F. Goodson and Stephen J. Ball, 89-115. London: Falmer Press, 1984.

## Magazines, newspapers, and journals

### Article in a popular magazine:
Mohr, Merilyn. "The Evolutionary Image." Equinox, March/April
    1989, 80-93.

### Article in a scholarly journal:
Creighton, D. G. "The Economic Background of the Rebellions of
    1867." The Canadian Journal of Economics and Political Science
    4 (1937): 322-34.

### Articles in encyclopedias:
Mohanty, Jitendra M. "Indian Philosophy." The New Encyclopedia
    Britannica: Macropedia. 15th ed. 1987.

### Newspaper:
"Feminists Demand Legal System Review." London Free Press, 10
    February 1990, D1.

### Book review:
Rugoff, Milton. "The Feminine Mystic." Review of Spiritualism and
    Women's Rights in Nineteenth Century America by Ann Braude.
    The New York Times Book Review, 14 Jan. 1990, 19.

## Non-print sources

### Motion picture:
Phillips, Robin. Dir. The Wars. Toronto: Spectra Films, 1983.

### Television or radio program:
CBC. "The Nature of Things." 7 February 1990. "Thirty Years of
    Discovery." David Suzuki, narrator.

### Published interview:
Davies, Robertson. "Interview with Robertson Davies: The Bizarre
    and Passionate Life of the Canadian People." Interview by Silver
    Donald Cameron (9 November 1971). Conversations with
    Canadian Novelists. Toronto: Colbert Agency, Inc., 1973.

### Unpublished interview:
Beedle, Merle Assance. Interview by author, March 1989.

## Special forms

### Unpublished materials:
Crown Attorney's Case Book for Cases Prosecuted Under the Liquor
    Control Act (1927) in Middlesex County. Regional Room, D. B.
    Weldon Library, University of Western Ontario, London.

### Dissertations:
Gates, David. "The Image of the Labyrinth in Some Victorian Novels."
    Ph.D. diss., The University of Western Ontario, 1982.

## Government Publications

Here are some basic rules to follow when citing government documents.

1. List name of country, state, city, or district first in bibliographies. In notes, however, this information may be left out because it will be obvious from the text.
2. Next, list the name of the legislative body, department, or board. Use the name of the office rather than the name of the officer.
3. Follow with the name of the division or commission, if any.
4. Give the title of the document, underlined.
5. Include any additional information needed to find the document.

*Use the following bibliographical format for a government publication:*

Issuing Body. Title. Personal Author. (Report number; medium).
    Edition. Place: Publisher, Date. (Series title, number).
Ontario. Commission on Planning and Development Reform in
    Ontario. New Planning for Ontario: Final Report. John Sewell.
    (Chair). Toronto: Queen's Printer for Ontario, 1993.

### Canadian documents:

List Canadian documents according to the executive department that issued them (either Senate or House of Commons). Identify them by calendar year. The note would also include chapter number.

Canada. House of Commons. Order Paper and Notices. 16 February
    1972.

Note Form:

[1] House of Commons, Order Paper and Notices, 16 February
1972, 6.

### American documents:

U. S. Congress. Senate. Committee on Foreign Relations. Aid
    Programs to Developing Countries. Washington, D.C.: GPO, 1989.

Here "GPO" stands for Government Printing Office.

Note Form:

[1] U. S. Congress, Senate, Committee on Foreign Relations, Aid
Programs to Developing Countries (Washington, D.C.: GPO, 1989), 7.

### British documents:

U. K. Board of Education. Report of the Committee on the Position of
    Natural Science in the Educational System of Great Britain.
    London: HMSO, 1918.

Here "HMSO" stands for Her (His) Majesty's Stationery Office.

Note Form:

¹ Board of Education, <u>Report of the Committee on the Position of Natural Science in the Educational System of Great Britain</u> (London: HMSO, 1918), 6.

For more help in citing government documents, refer to

Turabian, Kate L. <u>A Manual for Writers of Term Papers</u>. 5th ed. Chicago: University of Chicago Press, 1987.
Garner, Diane L., and Diane H. Smith. <u>Complete Guide to Citing Government Information Resources</u>. Rev. ed. Bethesda, Md.: Congressional Information Service, 1993.

# ■ Citing Sources in University of Chicago Style

Although notes can be used both for commentary and for reference, this section will concentrate on their use in making reference to particular works. Remember, though, that a note is often a good place to include supplementary commentary that does not belong in your paper proper, but that needs to be included.

In the University of Chicago style of documentation, you include notes compiled at the bottom of pages (footnotes) or in a list compiled at the end of the paper (endnotes). Each entry in your notes should correspond to a number in the text of your paper. The note numbers should appear a half line above your text at the end of the passage you are quoting or paraphrasing. The first line of each note is indented eight spaces from the left margin.

When you use this traditional style of documentation, always single-space your notes, and leave a space between each one.

The first note should contain complete information about the location of the source. Be sure to include everything that your reader will need to find it. Take your information from the title page of the work in question. The order of information for the first note follows this format:

## For a first complete note, in this case a book

Note number above the line
Name of author(s) in formal order
Title and subtitle, if any, underlined
Name of editor or translator
Name of author of introduction, if different from author
Name or number of edition, if other than the first
Name of series in which book appears, with volume or number
Facts of publication, enclosed in parentheses:

(Place of publication: Name of publisher, Date of publication), Page number of citation

Sometimes some of these things will not apply to the text you are citing. Occasionally, too, some of the facts of publication may be missing. These may be supplied in square brackets, if you know them, or they may be indicated by these abbreviations:

n.p. meaning "no place" or "no publisher" or both
n.d. meaning "no date"

A first full reference to a book would look like this:

[6] Northrop Frye, The Great Code: The Bible and Literature (New York: Harcourt Brace Jovanovich, 1982), p. 117.

## For a first complete note, in this case an article

Follow this order for an article in a magazine or periodical:

Name of author(s)
Title of article in quotation marks
Name of periodical underlined
Volume number or issue
Publication date in parentheses
Page numbers, inclusive (These normally are not preceded by "p." for page or "pp." for pages, unless confusion is possible.)

A first full reference to an article would look like this:

[3] Peter Elbow, "Embracing Contraries in the Writing Process," College Composition and Communication, 35, 155-171.

Note that long quoted passages in University of Chicago style are single-spaced and indented five spaces.

Note that there are some significant differences between the format of notes and that of bibliographic entries.

1.  Notes are listed consecutively by number; bibliographic entries are listed alphabetically by last name of author. Hence, authors' names are not inverted in notes, though they are in bibliographies.
2.  In notes, items are usually separated with commas; in bibliographic entries, items are separated with periods.
3.  Notes include facts of publication in parentheses; bibliographic entries do not enclose this information in parentheses.
4.  Notes include the specific page references of the citation; bibliographic entries do not, though they do include the page range of journal articles, inclusive.

## Notes after the first full reference to a work

The best way to cite something after the first full reference is to include the following:

Author's last name
Shortened title of the work, maintaining key words without changing word order
Page number

*Note:* The use of Latin abbreviations such as Ibid. is now discouraged.

The second references to the book and article listed above would look like these:

⁷ Frye, <u>Code</u>, 133.
⁸ Elbow, "Embracing Contraries," 333.

Some instructors may allow you to dispense with a shortened version of the title and use just the author's last name and the page number. This method is used only if you are citing no more than one work by an author. In any case, check with your instructor first.

# Fit, Form, and Function

# The Sentence Simplified

To grammar even kings bow.

*Molière*

S ome fundamental understanding of the way a sentence is put together will help you analyze your style, eliminate grammatical errors, and punctuate more accurately. First, learn to differentiate the parts of a sentence.

When analyzing a sentence, always find the verb first. The verb is the part of the sentence that describes the action or the state of being. Next, find the subject: ask WHO or WHAT performed the action or is being described. Note that, usually, the subject appears before the verb.

## *Example*

*Dabney lost his nerve.*

What is the verb? (lost — an action)

What is the subject? *Who* or *what* lost his nerve? (Dabney)

*His haircut looks dreadful.*

What is the verb? (looks — a state of being)

What is the subject? *Who* or *what* looks dreadful? (His haircut)

The most common English sentence is made up of a subject, a verb, and an object, usually in that order.

## *Example*

*Sweetiepie, the chimpanzee, refused to eat the banana.*
   S                              V        O

*It threw its food on the floor of the cage.*
S  V     O

*It gave the zookeeper a nasty look.*
S  V        O

*Even chimpanzees lose their temper.*
      S          V         O

In each of these cases, the first noun or pronoun in the sentence is the subject, which performs the action. What follows the subject is the predicate, made up of the verb, which describes the action, and the object, which receives the action.

Another common simple sentence pattern is subject, verb, and complement, sometimes called a "subjective completion." Here the verb must be a linking verb that describes a state of being, rather than an action.

## *Example*

*Mary Jane is not a good dancer.*
    S      V         C

*She often seems clumsy.*
 S        V     C

*She appears unaware of her partner's dismay.*
 S    V      C

*Some people just don't look graceful.*
    S          V        C

A sentence is a grammatical unit that can stand alone. It must be composed of a subject and verb and is usually accompanied by an object or a complement.

## ■ Parts of Speech

A knowledge of the roles parts of speech play will help you understand how your sentences are constructed.

### Nouns

Nouns name something, a person, place, or thing. They may be abstract or concrete. As a general rule, something may be classified as a noun if you can put an article ("a," "an," or "the") or a possessive pronoun ("my," "her") in front of it.

## *Example*

| | |
|---|---|
| *advertising* | *corset* |
| *philosophy* | *computer* |
| *doctor* | *giraffe* |

### Pronouns

Pronouns stand in the place of nouns. There are many kinds of pronouns.

**Personal:** I, you, he, she, we, they (subjective)
                me, you, him, her, us, them (objective)
                my, your, his, her, our, their (possessive)
                mine, yours, his, hers, ours, theirs (absolute possessive)

*I never should have lent **her my** new flashlight.*

**Reflexive** or **Intensive**: myself, yourself, and so on

> *Frankenstein's creature was shocked when he looked at **himself** in the mirror.* (reflective)

> *I did it all by **myself**.* (intensive)

**Relative**: who, which, that, whose, whoever, whomever, whichever, and so on

> *The best friends are those **who** know when to keep quiet.*

These pronouns connect subordinate clauses to main clauses.

**Interrogative**: who, whom, which, what

> ***What** do you mean by that?*

These pronouns begin questions.

**Demonstrative**: this, that, these, those, such

> ***Such** is life.*

These pronouns point to someone or something.

**Indefinite**: any, some, each, every, few, everyone, everybody, someone, somebody

> ***Everybody** loves **somebody** sometime.*

These pronouns stand for an indefinite number of people or things.

**Reciprocal**: each other, one another

> *Scott and Zelda hated **each other** intensely.*

These pronouns express a reciprocal relationship.

## Verbs

A verb is an action word or a word that describes a state of being. It may have many forms and tenses. It also may be composed of an auxiliary verb and a main verb. Verbs may be transitive or intransitive (some verbs may be either), or linking.

A transitive verb needs an object to be complete.

> *Winston **shut** his mouth.*

An intransitive verb is complete without an object.

> *Rita **yawned**.*

A linking verb connects the subject to a state of being.

> *Malcolm **is** mischievous.*

# Adjectives

Adjectives describe or modify nouns.

## *Examples*

| | |
|---|---|
| *delicious* | *wooden* |
| *handsome* | *abstract* |
| *devilish* | *superstitious* |

# Adverbs

Adverbs describe or modify verbs, adjectives, and other adverbs. They often end in "ly."

## *Examples*

| | |
|---|---|
| *soon* | *too* |
| *devilishly* | *now* |
| *often* | *generally* |

# Prepositions

The preposition is a linking word that is always followed by a noun.

## *Examples*

| | |
|---|---|
| **on** *the wagon* | *according* **to** *her* |
| **in** *your mind* | **by** *all accounts* |
| **to** *the lifeboats* | **from** *me* **to** *you* |

# Conjunctions

Conjunctions are used to join two words, phrases, or clauses.

## *Examples*

*The office sent invoices to those **who** owed money **and** greeting cards to those **who** did not.*
***After** the war was over, Ashley returned to Melanie.*
*Love is **as** strong **as** death.*

# Interjections

Interjections are exclamatory words or phrases that interrupt a sentence.

## *Examples*

***No,** I don't want to go to the dentist.*
***My word!** I simply don't believe what you say.*

NOTE: Keep the following definitions in mind as you read the next chapter.

# Phrase

A phrase is a group of words.

*Examples*

playing doctor
in the tree house

## Clause

A clause is a group of words with a subject and a verb.

*Example*

We were playing doctor in the tree house.

# Common Sentence Problems

It's not wise to violate the rules until you know how to observe them.

*T.S. Eliot*

A well-structured sentence tells its readers where to start and where to stop. The sentence, if it is correctly formed, constitutes a complete thought. It contains a main subject and a main verb connected to the subject.

## ■ Sentence Structure

### Avoid fragments

A sentence fragment lacks either a subject or a main verb. Or, sometimes, it ignores the connection between them.

### *Example*

> ✗ *Ramona did not follow the cheesecake recipe. But added Cheddar instead of cream cheese.*

(missing subject: she)

> ✓ *Ramona did not follow the cheesecake recipe. She added Cheddar instead of cream cheese.*
> ✗ *Wilhelm enjoyed many forms of relaxation. Practising tai chi, doing origami, and baking cookies.*

(no connection to the subject: he)

> ✓ *Wilhelm enjoyed many forms of relaxation: practising tai chi, doing origami, and baking cookies.*
> ✗ *Norrie didn't bring his homework. Because Fido ate it.*
> ✓ *Norrie didn't bring his homework because Fido ate it.*

NOTE: A fragment may, on rare occasions, be used for rhetorical effect. Deliberate fragments must, however, be used sparingly. It is also a wise idea to use a dash (two hyphens in typing) before a deliberate sentence fragment to indicate its purpose to your reader.

*Example*

*Should colleges and universities have the right to charge foreign students higher tuition than native-born students? — Under no circumstances.*

## Avoid run-on sentences

A run-on sentence is actually two sentences that run together without any punctuation to indicate where one ends and the next begins.

*Example*

✗ *Hedda couldn't sleep on the new waterbed she always felt seasick.*
✓ *Hedda couldn't sleep on the new waterbed. She always felt seasick.*

## Avoid comma splices

A comma splice is similar to a run-on sentence. It occurs when two main clauses are "spliced," or incorrectly joined, by a comma. The comma splice fails to show the relationship between two clauses.

*Example*

✗ *Graeme had too much to drink, he got the hiccups.*
✗ *His mother was the designated driver, she took him home.*

A comma splice, like a visible seam, is a sign of faulty workmanship. There are several methods by which it may be corrected. Run-ons may also be treated the same way:

1.  **Join the two ideas with one of the following co-ordinating conjunctions: and, or, nor, for, but, yet, so.**

*Example*

✓ *Graeme had too much to drink, and he got the hiccups.*
✓ *His mother was the designated driver, so she took him home.*

2.  **Join the two ideas with a subordinating conjunction.**

*Example*

✓ *Because Graeme had too much to drink, he got the hiccups.*
✓ *Since his mother was the designated driver, she took him home.*

3.  **Form two separate sentences.**

*Example*

✓ *Graeme had too much to drink. He got the hiccups.*
✓ *His mother was the designated driver. She took him home.*

4.  **Join the two ideas with a semicolon.**

Use this method of correction only if the two ideas in question are logically connected. Note that sometimes a word may be used as a conjunctive adverb to join two sentences with a semicolon. Such words as "however," "therefore," and "hence" frequently serve this function. For more information, see page 163.

## *Example*

✓ *Graeme had too much to drink; he got the hiccups.*
✓ *His mother was the designated driver; she took him home.*

## CHAPTER 16 EXERCISE A

Correct the comma splices, run-ons, and fragments in these sentences. Some may be correct as they are. Answers begin on p. 201.

1. The customer found the jalapeño peppers in the gumbo too hot, he drank two pitchers of water during dinner.

2. The audience disliked the new play, they clearly felt that the director's talents did not lie in playwriting.

3. All the members of his family lacked inner resources they sought constant stimulation and would never dream of picking up a book.

4. The children begged their father to buy a golden Labrador retriever, he soon became a much-loved part of the household and a symbol of domestic harmony.

5. The neighbours objected to the new apartment building development, city hall ignored their complaints and went ahead with the project anyway.

6. On the eighteenth floor, it can get rather windy, all the dust bunnies come out when there is a storm.

7. In Aristophanes' *Clouds*, a comic look at education, students destroying the university.

8. *The Dilbert Principle*, a non-fiction bestseller, exploring how good employees get fired and bad employees get, ironically, promoted.

9. After four job interviews across North America, Sally Jo built up enough travel points to buy dinner for two in a fancy restaurant.

10. Geoffrey grew a beard this past summer it hid his double chin.

## CHAPTER 16 EXERCISE B

Correct the comma splices, run-ons, and fragments in these sentences. Some may be correct as they are. Check your answers on p. 201.

1. Thelma bought a new convertible, the other one had been in an accident when she visited the Grand Canyon.

2. Poetry was Mei Ling's passion, cleaning house was her life.

3. Felix, Emily's cat, was demoralized by a raccoon he was taken to the vet but released when the doctor failed to find a scratch on him.

4. Mimi distinguished herself when she wrote the entrance exam, she was probably the only candidate who wore a mink coat.

5. Jake liked souvenirs, he owned more fridge magnets, mugs, and rude postcards than anyone in the country.

6. Life in the residence upset Della, she missed her microwave, her privacy, and her cats.

7. Teresa didn't believe in career counsellors instead she made a lot of appointments with psychics.

8. Cindy Lou hated public transit, on her most recent bus trip she sat beside a fellow who laughed uncontrollably, for no apparent reason, every few minutes.

9. Mabel's experiences as an announcer on the local radio program making her wish that she could become a media celebrity.

10 Being excitable, Ginger, my terrier, greeting guests by jumping up and down at the screen door.


# ■ Modifiers

Modifiers are descriptive words or phrases. A modifier may be a simple adverb or an adjective, or a more complex adverbial phrase or adjectival phrase. A modifier should describe clearly and unambiguously. To do so, it must be as near in the sentence as possible to the thing described.

## Avoid misplaced modifiers

A modifier, whether a word or a phrase, should be placed next to the word it describes.

### Examples
___

*✗ Emmylou chased the mouse carrying a knife.*
*✓ Carrying a knife, Emmylou chased the mouse.*
*✗ Licking each other fondly, the children admired the kittens.*
*✓ Licking each other fondly, the kittens were admired by the children.*

## Watch the position of limiting modifiers

A limiting modifier is a word that qualifies part or all of the statement. Consider carefully the placement of the following modifiers (and others): only, just, nearly, almost, hardly.

### Examples
___

*Only Gilbert brought a case of beer.*

(No one else brought one.)

*Gilbert brought only a case of beer.*

(He brought only one case.)

*Gilbert brought a case of beer only.*

(He didn't bring a case of wine.)

## Avoid squinting modifiers

A squinting modifier is ambiguously placed in the sentence, so that the writer's intention is unclear.

*Examples*
_____

*The suspect confessed that he had served time **later**.*
*The suspect confessed **later** that he had served time.*

## Avoid dangling modifiers

A modifier dangles when what it is meant to describe is accidentally left out of the sentence. To figure out what it does describe, ask WHO or WHAT is being described.

*Examples*
_____

✗ *After vacuuming the living-room rug, the cat tracked mud all over it.*
✓ *After vacuuming the living-room rug, I saw that the cat had tracked mud all over it.*

OR

✓ *After I vacuumed the living-room rug, the cat tracked mud all over it.*

Dangling modifiers that end in "ing" are usually easy to spot. Remember, however, that a dangling modifier may also involve a prepositional phrase or an infinitive form. A dangling modifier may also occur at the end of a sentence.

*Examples*
_____

✗ *As a weightlifter, my muscles are in tremendous shape.*
✓ *As a weightlifter, I believe that my muscles are in tremendous shape.*
✗ *To get a high-paying job, education is essential.*
✓ *To get a high-paying job, you need education.*
✗ *Fernando's travel bills were expensive, being used to flying first class.*
✓ *Being used to flying first class, Fernando had expensive travel bills.*

OR

✓ *Since Fernando was used to flying first class, his travel bills were expensive.*

Note that some modifiers apply to the entire sentence rather than to any one word or phrase within it. These constructions, called "absolute modifiers," include phrases such as "To make a long story short" and "All things considered."

## CHAPTER 16 EXERCISE A

Correct the modifier problems in the following sentences. Some may be correct as they stand. Answers begin on p. 202.

1. Travelling on the bus late at night, the sound of a passenger's maniacal laughter alarmed Jamie.

2. Living in the penthouse apartment in a high-rise, it can be inconvenient when the power goes off.

3. When carrying a notebook computer, inspiration may strike at any time.

4. To accomplish everything on her gruelling schedule, late nights, stamina, and many cups of coffee are essential.

5. Deepak almost gave up on finding a wheelchair-accessible entrance, but by persevering and seeking help from strangers, he was able to get into the building.

6. Recovering from last night's party, a quiet morning and a liquid breakfast seemed appealing to Doris and Russell.

7. Not pleased by the recent loss of his job, *Dilbert* comic strips became Tom's passion.

8. The retiring employees were only interested in the size of their pensions, not in the company's plans for a corporate takeover.

9. Not owning the latest computer equipment, Steven's contributions to the project consisted of handwritten notes.

10. After conducting a feasibility study, it was determined that the easiest way to make money was to buy a parking lot.

## CHAPTER 16 EXERCISE B

Correct the modifier problems in the following sentences.

1. Tessa killed the cockroach with a mop scurrying across the floor.

2. To impress your new boss, arriving on time is a good idea.

3. Gabled and surrounded by beautiful trees and shrubs, the professor had his home declared a heritage property.

4. Freddie saw the vineyard taking the regional wine tour.

5. Freddie saw the vineyard while taking the regional wine tour.

6. As a taxpayer, the right to attend meetings at city hall is something I believe in.

7. After dropping a book on his toe, Geoffrey's ability to get to class on time was severely affected.

8. Asleep at the wheel, the car and its occupant rolled into the ditch; he escaped injury.

9. Giovanni only buys tomato sandwiches in the cafeteria, as a dedicated vegetarian.

10. Working out frequently in the gym, James's physique improved dramatically.

# ■ Pronoun Reference and Agreement

A pronoun, as the name suggests, acts for a noun, or in the place of a noun. A pronoun should almost always refer to a specific noun in the sentence itself. The noun to which it refers is called an "antecedent." When a pronoun does not refer clearly to its antecedent, confusing or ambiguous writing is the result.

## A guide to proper pronoun usage

Make sure your pronoun matches its antecedent. A pronoun must agree in gender: it may be masculine (he, him, his), feminine (she, her, hers), or neuter (it, it, its). A pronoun must also agree in number: it may be singular or plural.

## In gender

### Examples

> *Nancy named **her** dachshund Simon.*
> *Nancy named **him** Simon.*

In the second sentence, "her dachshund" has been replaced by the masculine pronoun "him."

In the past, the masculine pronouns ("he," "his," "him") were used to refer generally to nouns that were not specifically feminine.

### Example

> *The reader must make up **his** own mind.*

Although the masculine pronoun is still, strictly speaking, grammatically correct, many people now find its general use offensive. It is now more common to find such cases phrased as

> *The reader must make up **his or her** own mind.*

For those who find the use of "his or her" cumbersome, the best solution is to use the plural pronoun, and an accompanying plural noun, of course.

### Example

> *Readers must make up **their** own minds.*

The determination of gender in English does not pose much of a problem, apart from this dispute. Problems do arise, however, with the number of pronouns.

## In number

**1.  Be sure to locate the correct antecedent for the pronoun in question.**

## Example

*Chloë is one of those students **who** skip their classes regularly.*

"Students" is the antecedent of the relative pronoun WHO. Both the verb "skip" and the pronoun "their" are plural. Note that "one of those" takes the plural, but "one of these" is singular, as in one of these gloves is lost.

## 2. Be especially careful with collective nouns and their pronoun replacements.

When a collective noun is considered as a unit, the pronoun that stands for it is singular.

## Example

*The jury has reached its decision.*

Here the jury acts as a unit.
When the component parts of a collective noun are considered individually, the pronoun that stands for it is plural.

## Example

*The jury have expressed their differences of opinion.*

Here the jury acts individually; each member has his or her own opinion.

## 3. Be careful of imprecise use of some indefinite pronouns.

"Anyone," "anybody," "someone," "somebody," "everyone," "everybody," "each," "either," "neither," "nobody," and "no one" are indefinite pronouns, all of which generally take singular verbs.

## Example

*Nobody wore his or her bathing suit.*

Ideally, "his or her" should allow an indefinite pronoun, if the construction is to avoid charges of sexism. In conversation, many people would get around this problem by saying,

*Nobody wore their bathing suits.*

This form, despite its regular occurrence in spoken English, is still considered imprecise grammatically. It should properly be replaced by the following:

*None of us wore our bathing suits.*

The best approach is to use the plural form.

## In case

Pronouns, besides being masculine or feminine, singular or plural, also have different forms, depending on their case. They may be used as subjects ("he," "she," "they"), objects ("him," "her," "them"), or possessives ("his," "her," "their").

1. **Use the subjective form if the pronoun is the subject of a verb (stated or implied).**

*Example*

> The police officer stated that it was **she** who had reported the theft of the painting.

"She" is used here because a verb is implied.

> It was **they** who had masterminded the heist.

"They" and not "them" is used here because it functions as the subject of the verb "had masterminded."

This precision is essential in writing English, but in informal speech, by contrast, "It's me" or "It was her" is considered acceptable.

2. **Make sure to use the objective form of the pronoun if it is the object of a verb.**

*Example*

> The poodle gave his master fleas.
> The poodle gave **him them.**

In the second version, the objective forms for both pronouns — objects of the verb "gave" — have been substituted.

> The poodle gave **his master and me** fleas.

Although you might be tempted to write "The poodle gave his master and I fleas," it becomes obvious that the objective pronoun "me" is correct when you remove the words "his master and." When the pronoun case is a problem, try taking out part of a compound subject and reading the sentence. The correct pronoun should then be obvious.

3. **Make sure to use the objective form of the pronoun if it is the object of a preposition.**

*Example*

> Between **you** and **me**, I think you should use deodorant.
> It's important for **you** and **me** to wear clean underwear every day.

4. **After "than" or "as," use the form of the pronoun that would be required in the complete implied clause.**

*Examples*

> A sloth is harder working than **he** [is].
> A monkey can communicate as well as **she** [can].

Note the difference in meaning in the following examples:

> I love you as much as **he** [does].
> I love you as much as [I love] **him.**

# ■ Pronoun Problems in Essay Writing

## Use personal pronouns with discretion

Too few personal references in an essay may be as awkward as too many. Few instructors disallow the use of "I" entirely. Its occasional use should prevent needless circumlocution and impersonality. Never stoop to cold and formal constructions like "It is the opinion of this writer," or the overly polite "myself." "We" is sometimes acceptable, though its overuse may sound pompous. "One" may serve as an alternative, though it runs the risk of sounding too distanced and impersonal.

You are writing your paper: its words and thoughts are yours. Avoid "I" and "in my opinion" only when a personal perspective might make your point seem weak or merely a matter of personal idiosyncrasy.

## Check to see that your pronoun references are present and accounted for

> UNCLEAR: In small towns, they do not lock their cars.
> CLEARER: Residents of small towns do not lock their cars.
>
> UNCLEAR: Esther changed the baby's diaper, and it screamed.
> CLEARER: When Esther changed its diaper, the baby screamed.
>
> UNCLEAR: Robert hates studying floristry, but he intends to become one anyway.
> CLEARER: Robert hates studying floristry, but he intends to become a florist anyway.

## Avoid broad pronoun references

A broad pronoun reference occurs when "this," "which," or "that" is used to refer to an idea rather than to a specific word in the sentence. Some broad references may be tolerated, if the meaning is generally clear. Be careful of raising unanswered questions in the reader's mind, however.

> UNCLEAR: Dexter stays up all night watching reruns of "Leave It to Beaver," which is why he falls asleep on the job so often.
> CLEARER: Dexter stays up all night watching reruns of "Leave It to Beaver," a habit which causes him to fall asleep on the job often.

"Which" does not clearly refer to any specific noun in the preceding sentence. Add a noun before "which" to clarify the point.

---

## CHAPTER 16 EXERCISE A

Correct the usage of the pronouns in the following sentences. Some may be correct as they stand. Check your answers on p. 203.

1. On the menu, it says that someone who's allergies to certain foods present a problem may be specially accommodated by the chef.

2. As for myself, I don't believe in relying on hypnosis for the answers to one's problems. They assume that all one's problems are in your head.

3. To honour the occasion, the guests brought tacky shower presents for her and I; we received it as graciously as possible, all the while wondering what we would do with all the kites and balloons.

4. Everyone who we invited to the meeting had their own definite ideas about how to make more money.

5. Each of the candidates for public office were vague about their platform; that way, they wouldn't have to back down later.

6. Emilio stepped on the lizard's tail, and it hissed at him.

7. In the bestseller *Chicken Soup for the Soul*, it tells stories of how people overcame adversity and triumphed over their circumstances.

8. I was just as angry as her when I found out that the door to the classroom was locked; of course, her and I both had to find a custodian to let us in.

9. When a hockey player gets a penalty, everyone on the team suffers because of them.

10. Just between you and I, his mother and him were shocked to discover that the school intended to close washrooms as a cost-cutting measure.

## CHAPTER 16 EXERCISE B

Correct the usage of the pronouns in the following sentences. Some may be correct as they stand. Answers are on p. 203–204.

1. Patricia had a wonderful idea for a business; in her feasibility study, it said that what this country needs is a school for fools.

2. The tradition of the fool as the servant of powerful people exists in Shakespeare's work; Pat wondered if they could not become a useful part of the modern economy as well.

3. The fool, according to Shakespeare, was often wise; they performed the useful social function of the moral conscience to the king.

4. If one were to imagine a chief executive officer in a large corporation, rather than a king, you might begin to appreciate how marketable this idea could become.

5. Graduates with sharp wits who's education has provided them with access to much-quoted wisdom would have an edge in the job market.

6. Powerful people would be willing to hire fools like me and her, Pat argued, just as they are now willing to hire personal trainers, administrative assistants, and other advisers.

7. The study which Pat wrote is liable to be considered a joke by some, but frankly, I think a fool might become a status symbol for the rich. He or she would be hiring their own personal stand-up comedian.

8. Whom do you suppose would be willing to admit that he wanted to be trained as a fool?

9. Each of the candidates for the course would be subjected to an audition to find out if they were able to make an audience laugh about human foibles.

10. Both Pat and me believe that there may be some stigma attached to the occupation of the fool; being funny, between you and I, is not really respectable, for some reason.

## Subject and Verb Agreement

The subject and verb in a sentence are closely connected. In order for the sentence to express itself clearly, the subject and the verb must agree.

Most problems with agreement between subject and verb result from difficulties in locating the subject of a verb. Solve these problems by locating the verb in each clause. Remember, first, that a verb describes either an action or a state of being. Next, ask WHO or WHAT is performing that action or is being described. The answer to the question WHO or WHAT is the subject of the verb. Having located the subject and verb, you may then check to see that they match.

### Example

> Big Brother is watching you.

WHO is watching?
— Big Brother (the subject of the verb "is watching")

### How to match subjects and verbs correctly

Check to see that verbs agree in number with their subjects. In other words, singular subjects take singular verbs; plural subjects take plural verbs.

**Problems to watch for:**

**1. The noun that immediately precedes the verb may not be the subject.**

### Example

> Not one of these science-fiction writers has ever seen an extra-terrestrial creature.

The correct subject is "one."

**2. Subjects joined by "and" are usually, but not always, plural.**

### Example

> My friend and guardian angel has come to my rescue.

"My friend and guardian angel" refers to one person.

**3. Singular subjects that are joined by a phrase other than "and" are not made plural. Such phrases as "as well as," "in addition to," and "along with" have no effect on the agreement of the verb since they are not part of the subject.**

*Example*

---

*A hamburger, along with french fries, is Dee's typical dinner.*

"Along with french fries" is not part of the subject.

**4. Subjects joined by "or" or "nor" are each considered separately. The verb agrees with the subject closest to it.**

*Example*

---

*Neither tears nor litigation moves Scrooge to act fairly toward his employees.*

"Tears" and "litigation" are each considered separately; since "litigation" is closer, the verb is singular.

**5. The following subjects always take singular verbs: "each," "either," "neither," "one," and words ending in "body" or "one."**

*Example*

---

*Neither of the twins eats turnip.*

**6. Subjects like "some," "all," "most," "any," or "none" may take singular or plural verbs, depending upon the noun to which they refer.**

*Examples*

---

*Some of the guests refuse to eat parsnip.*
*All of us enjoy caviar.*

(plural verb)

*All of the caviar is gone.*

(singular verb)

**7. A collective noun, used to refer to a group of people or things, takes a singular verb when the collective is considered as a unit and a plural verb when each member is considered individually.**

*Example*

---

Singular (considered a unit): *The union is planning a strike.*

Plural (considered as individuals within the group): *The union are voting on the new benefits package.*

**8. A linking verb (a verb describing a state of being) agrees with its subject and not with its predicate.**

*Example*

---

*The only thing Myrna ever buys is cigarettes.*

"Thing" is the subject; hence, "is" is the appropriate verb.

*Cigarettes are the only thing Myrna ever buys.*

In this example, "cigarettes" is the subject; hence, the plural verb is correct.

**9. A verb still agrees with its subject, even when their order is inverted. The subject follows "there is" or "there are," "here is" or "here are," and the verb is singular or plural accordingly.**

*Example*

*Here are the pizzas you ordered.*

Here "pizzas" is the subject; hence, the correct verb is "are."

**10. Relative pronouns (who, which, that), acting as subjects, take singular or plural verbs, depending on the words to which they refer (their antecedents).**

*Example*

*Harry is one of those people who cheat at Scrabble.*

"People," the antecedent of "who," is plural; hence, the verb "cheat" is also plural.

BUT NOTE:

*Harry is the only one of us who spells badly.*

"One" is the antecedent in this case; hence, the verb "spells" is singular.

**11. Some nouns may look plural though they are actually singular. Examples include "physics," "economics," "ethics," and "news." Check doubtful usage in a dictionary.**

*Example*

*News is big business on television today.*

---

## CHAPTER 16 EXERCISE A

Correct the agreement between subject and verb in the following sentences. Check your answers on p. 204.

1. Sigrid, together with Kim, spend all the time painting, taking photographs, and watching videotapes of old movies.

2. Neither a borrower nor a lender are likely to befriend Brad after his latest entrepreneurial scheme.

3. The cost of the fax machine as well as the laser printer were prohibitive; the employees used the phone and wrote in pencil to save money.

4. There is a number of good reasons to buy a sofa bed: air mattresses are inconvenient and hardwood floors are hard on the back.

5. Defending family values and marketing children's services was Dustin's job as the new publicist.

6. The price of curtains seem extravagantly high, so his cousins decided to keep the windows bare.

7. Every single one of us have been nervous before a job interview, especially when we have been faced with a group of intimidating questioners.

8. The only thing Bryan works at is building up his muscles so that he can be the strongest person in the trailer park.

9. The vitamin supplement, along with the bee pollen, are meant to keep your energy levels high.

10. On the hard drive, unbeknownst to anyone, was a letter Leah had written to her brother and a diary of her innermost thoughts.

---

**CHAPTER 16 EXERCISE B**

Correct the agreement between subject and verb in the following sentences.
Answers are on p. 205.

1. At the bottom of Edwina's purse among her credit card receipts was a tiny bottle of vodka and a couple of straws.

2. A series of shocking crimes have been recently reported to the newspaper hot line.

3. Either Phil or Gwynneth make hors d'oeuvres for the guests at the book club.

4. Spike, with his new tools and his powersaw, enjoy doing handy jobs around the house.

5. The fireworks on New Year's Eve was appreciated by all except the birds that inhabited the sycamore tree behind the house.

6. Neither Ross nor Barbra are available to answer the telephone at present.

7. The lack of jobs, along with an increase in consumer debt, have led to reduced spending.

8. Floor stripper, along with many cleaning solvents, are highly inflammable.

9. Travels to a previously unknown destination leads to creativity sometimes, as it did in the case of *Midnight in the Garden of Good and Evil* or *A Year in Provence*.

10. Jim's bad eating habits and unimaginative routine was his downfall.

# ■ End Punctuation

## 1. Use a period after a statement, an indirect question, or a command.

### *Examples*

*I have something to tell you.* (statement)

*Don't look now.* (command)

*Penny asked me when I got my nose fixed.* (indirect question)

2. Use a period after most abbreviations, unless they are easily recognized. Note that some formal abbreviations, such as Mr., Mrs., and Dr., always end with a period in common usage.

*Examples*

| | |
|---|---|
| *Mr.* | *CBC* |
| *Mrs.* | *VCR* |
| *Dr.* | *CD player* |

3. Use a question mark after a direct question.

*Examples*

*Who's been eating my porridge?*
*Whatever is the matter?*
*What's for supper?*

4. Use exclamation marks sparingly to express emphasis, in an informal essay. Use them in a formal essay at your own risk.

*Example*

✗ *Hugo did his homework!*
✓ *Amazingly, Hugo did his homework.*

## ■ The Colon

The colon (:) is used to introduce something. Remember the following rules for colon usage:

1. Use a colon only after a complete sentence (that is, after an independent clause).

*Example*

✗ *Delores loved: foreign vacations, fur coats, and cold cash.*
✓ *Delores loved three things: foreign vacations, fur coats, and cold cash.*

2. Use a colon after a complete sentence to introduce ideas, lists, or quotations.

*Examples*

*Lucy van Pelz wants only one thing for Christmas: real estate.*
*Bette Midler makes this claim: "The worst part of success is to try finding someone who is happy for you."*

3. Use a colon to indicate amplification or further development of an idea.

*Example*

*Thanatology is a branch of psychology: it deals with the subject of death and dying.*

# ◼ The Semicolon

A semicolon (;) is a heavier punctuation mark than a comma, but lighter than a period. Use a semicolon generally only where you might use a period instead.

Semicolons are especially useful in the following cases:

### 1. Use a semicolon to join two closely related main clauses.

The use of a semicolon instead of a co-ordinating conjunction shows a close connection (or a sharp antithesis) between two ideas.

### Example

> Man proposes; God disposes.

### 2. Use a semicolon with a transitional word or phrase when it is used to join two main clauses.

Transitional words or phrases such as "however," "moreover," "furthermore," "hence," "as a result," and "consequently" may be used in this way.

### Example

> I won't accept charity; however, I will take cash or travellers' cheques.

The semicolon takes the place of a period in this sentence.

BUT NOTE:

> I will not, however, accept charity.

In this case, "however" is not used to join two main clauses. Since the transitional word interrupts one main clause, commas are adequate punctuation.

### 3. Use a semicolon to separate items listed in a series, if commas are already used as internal punctuation.

### Example

> Maxwell always did three things before he went to bed: one, he put on his pyjamas; two, he drank warm milk; three, he fell asleep in the armchair in front of the TV set.

## CHAPTER 16 EXERCISE A

Add, remove, or substitute colons or semicolons in the following sentences. (Sometimes lighter punctuation, like a comma, may also be used instead.) Some may be correct as they stand. Check your answers on p. 205.

1. When her friends recommended hypnotism as a good way to break a bad habit, Briar was afraid she would wind up clucking like a chicken, however, she decided to give it a try.

2. The doctor assured her that people were not supposed to fall asleep, instead they remained conscious throughout the entire session.

3. As she soon discovered, like her, many people were nervous at the thought of being hypnotized; mainly because they feared losing control.

4. Briar wanted to give up biting her nails; a habit which she considered unsightly; and she enlisted the hypnotist's help to do that.

5. In a post-hypnotic suggestion, the doctor warned her that her nails would now seem to have a dreadful, bitter taste: that she would find repulsive.

6. He included: that she would become gradually more interested in manicures and hand-care products.

7. In addition, he made this subliminal suggestion on a tape: that she would keep her hands busy by knitting compulsively; whenever she felt an urge to chew her nails.

8. Briar knew that health insurance would probably not cover the cost of a hypnotist; but she felt she would benefit anyway: false nails are expensive; so are Band-Aids.

9. Now Briar's nails are as long as Barbra Streisand's, for some reason; she can't seem to stop knitting; however.

10. She doesn't cluck like a chicken; though now she can scratch like one.

---

## CHAPTER 16 EXERCISE B

Add, remove, or substitute colons or semicolons in the following sentences. (Sometimes lighter punctuation, like a comma, may also be used instead.) Some may be correct as they stand. Answers are on p. 206.

1. Commuting is a challenge to the strongest nerves, despite the weather, every day a driver must gear up for a journey that culminates in one rather unappealing thing: work.

2. People who commute regularly start to play mind games, some claim they have named all the trees along the route.

3. Car pools can help defray the cost of gasoline and provide some much-needed company for the person behind the wheel; better still, people can share the driving.

4. Hazards like flat tires are common; so it is wise to carry a car phone or at least flares: to alert other travellers.

5. If you are inclined, you may invest in motivational tapes or talking books; which will educate or, at any rate, distract you along the way.

6. Despite the temptation, commuters should not talk on the car phone; apply make-up; or comb their hair while driving.

7. Speeding tickets are another hazard; avoid a "heavy foot" when you feel pressed for time, if not, you will pay a fine, and your insurance rates will rise substantially.

8. Commuters should get a good night's sleep, when you are drowsy, you can stop for coffee at one of Canada's ubiquitous doughnut shops.

9. If you have to commute long distances, try to find a scenic route to dull the monotony occasionally; repetition is tedious and may lull you to sleep.

10. When you do get caught in traffic; however, relax; listen to the radio, and don't yell at other drivers.

## ■ The Comma

A comma (,) is a light mark of punctuation. Some basic rules that govern its use are listed below. When in doubt about a particular usage, let ease in reading be your guide.

### 1. Use a comma before "and," "or," "nor," "for," "but," "yet," "so," if any of these words are used to join two independent clauses.

*Example*

*Gunther doesn't normally snore, but tonight his dog needs earplugs.*

BUT NOTE:
A comma should not be used if a complete independent clause does not follow.

*Example*

*Ivor hates school but loves recess.*

In this case, "but" actually joins a compound verb, rather than two independent clauses.

### 2. You may use a comma after a word, a phrase, or a clause used to introduce the main subject and verb. The comma is essential if the sentence would be confusing without it.

*Examples*

*Bracing himself, Rocky applied for a job as a snake charmer.*
*Because he had never seen a snake before, Rocky was different from the other candidates.*
*Alas, the snake did not find him charming enough.*

### 3. Use a comma after a word or phrase that modifies an entire sentence. To find out whether something is a sentence modifier, test to see if it can be moved elsewhere in the sentence without changing the meaning.

*Example*

*However, he did find work cleaning cages at the zoo.*

"However" can be shifted in the sentence; hence, it is a sentence modifier.

*He did, however, find work cleaning cages at the zoo.*

## 4. Use a comma for the sake of contrast before an antithetical element.

*Examples*

> Tracy attended school for the social life, not for the good of her mind.
> Pee-Wee wanted precious antiques, but found worthless junk.

## 5. Use commas to separate elements in a series.

*Examples*

> Cinderella invited Flora, Fauna, and Merryweather to her coming-out party.

A comma before "and" at the end of the list is usually advisable to prevent confusion.

> Ogden tells us that his old age begins, and middle age ends, and now his descendants outnumber his friends.

Here a comma is used to separate a series of independent clauses. Note, however, that two independent clauses together must normally be separated by a semicolon.

## 6. Put commas around words, phrases, or clauses that interrupt a sentence. Commas may be used around a word or a group of words if that part of the sentence might be removed and still leave a subject and predicate.

*Examples*

> Frankly, my dear, I am indifferent.
> Yes, Virginia, there is a Santa Claus.

## 7. Put commas around appositives, words that rename those that precede.

*Examples*

> Jethro and Elly May, Melissa's pet gerbils, are on the loose again.
> Madame de Pompadour said that Canada, then a colony of France, was useful only to provide her with furs.

## 8. Put commas around interrupting phrases or clauses that are non-restrictive in meaning.

*Examples*

> My grandmother, who lives in Los Angeles, is getting a divorce.

Here the clause "who lives in Los Angeles" is non-restrictive, and it implies that the author has one grandmother; some incidental information about her is enclosed in commas.

BUT NOTE:

> My grandmother who lives in Los Angeles is getting a divorce.

Here the clause "who lives in Los Angeles" is restrictive and lacks commas. It implies that the author has two grandmothers and uses the clause to identify which one.

**9. Commas should not enclose material that is restrictive, that is, essential to the sentence's meaning.**

*Example*

    ✗ *People, who live in glass houses, shouldn't throw stones.*

This sentence, because of the way it is punctuated, says that all people shouldn't throw stones.

    ✓ *People who live in glass houses shouldn't throw stones.*

This statement identifies those people who shouldn't throw stones. The modifier, because it performs the necessary function of identification or limitation, cannot be surrounded by commas.

**10. Commas should not separate main sentence elements. Do not use a comma between a subject and verb or between a verb and an object or complement.**

*Example*

    ✗ *Everything Zsa Zsa does, gets on my nerves.*
    ✓ *Everything Zsa Zsa does gets on my nerves.*

## CHAPTER 16 EXERCISE A

Add, remove, or substitute commas in the following sentences. Some may be fine as they are. Check your answers on p. 206.

1. Some cities in northern areas of Canada like Saskatoon have wide roads; something that allows for ease in snow removal.

2. As several members of the press noted the radiator in Greg's office admittedly old and in need of repair emitted a strange odour, and seemed unlikely to produce any heat.

3. Derk her imaginary friend, surprised everyone by turning up at the dinner party with a bottle of ice wine some panettone and some catnip for the hostess's pets to which he was allergic.

4. If Dave Broadfoot had six months to live he would move to Dundas Ontario for he claims that six months there would feel like five years anywhere else.

5. When one of the new employees refused to evacuate the building during a fire drill Regina the new chief executive officer was not impressed so she decided to make an example of her.

6. Annie the new director expressed astonishment that the former house manager and the erstwhile publicist both long since working at better jobs would dare to set foot in the old theatre even in a spirit of nostalgia.

7. When he was told how well he was looking Tyrone shocked that anyone would be impressed by his appearance backed up held up one hand smiled and asked "How many fingers am I holding up?" as if he were an optometrist.

8. Although the car was nicely warmed up and he was just about to cross the city limits Bradley was alarmed that he had left Hilary behind alone asleep and surrounded by paperwork in her office.

9. The most important job skill in the nineties is the ability to pack up the belongings in your office at a moment's notice.

10. Although Sean Connery on his way to a nearby golf course was rumoured to have been sighted on the elevator neither Jocasta nor Clytemnestra managed to get a glimpse of him.

## CHAPTER 16 EXERCISE B

Add, remove, or substitute commas in the following sentences. Some may be fine as they are. Answers are on p. 207.

1. Lawsuits that are launched by disgruntled employees patients and customers are often discussed in the papers lately but some of us feel that revenge is a dish best eaten cold.

2. Selling Ray's house turned out to be an ordeal, because the neighbours objected to the rezoning and the termites put off prospective buyers.

3. For reasons she could not entirely fathom the boss perhaps jealous because of her financial success told people that she made too much money; in fact Delores began to wonder if that was the reason for her job loss.

4. If you are feeling bored perhaps you should get Martha to teach you how to make gilt Easter eggs decorate your house with wildflowers culled from the roadside or give a party for seventy-five of your closest friends.

5. During the winter in cities like Victoria and Vancouver snow can create problems; you see hardly anyone keeps a shovel on hand.

6. Russians drink toasts to celebrate the simple joys of life; hence Melanie discovered the joys of vodka when she stayed with a family in Minsk.

7. Emily was not superstitious in the slightest so against the best advice of her parents she decided to name her first child Elektra.

8. Laughing hysterically Malo imagined Aloha his new puppy dancing to amuse the tourists.

9. The server claiming she had a hotel to run refused to seat them indoors when it began to rain: as a result the restaurant reviewer trashed the place severely in print.

10. Marie who had always wanted to be a pirate dreamed of starting a pirate school; in fact she planned to teach courses while wearing an eye patch swearing and carrying a parrot on her shoulder.

# ■ The Dash

Type a dash using two hyphens, with no spaces before or after.

*Example*

*I won't drink – – I want to know when I'm having a good time.*

**1. Use a dash for emphasis around parenthetical expressions.**

*Example*

*The show – – though a huge success with the public – – was panned by the critics.*

Note: Commas are also correct in this sentence, but less emphatic.

**2. Use a dash to introduce something with extra emphasis.**

*Example*

*Rob loved birthday cards – – whether cheques were enclosed or not.*

Note: A colon is also correct in this sentence but less emphatic.

**3. Keep the dash in reserve for special occasions. Use it sparingly, especially in formal writing.**

# ■ Parentheses

Parentheses are used to enclose incidental material. They (that is, the words they enclose) serve the same function as an aside in a theatrical production. Though they get the reader's attention, the material they enclose is presented as "inside information."

**1. Use parentheses in formal writing to enclose the necessary definition of a term at its first appearance.**

*Example*

*The NFB (National Film Board of Canada) has won several Academy Awards for its productions.*

**2. Use parentheses to enclose any part of a sentence that might be enclosed by commas or dashes, if the reader has only passing interest in it.**

*Example*

*In the next episode of "Degrassi Junior High" (Saturday night at nine), the twins seek a cure for acne.*

3. **Use parentheses sparingly. Too many make the writing self-conscious and hard to follow.**

*Example*

---

✗ *In this report (which is the product of months of arduous research), I will discuss various methods of sleep-teaching.*

## ■ Possession

Apostrophes are used after nouns and indefinite pronouns (e.g., "anyone," "somebody") to indicate possession. Note these general rules:

1. **Add " 's" to form the possessive case if the owner is singular.**

*Examples*

---

*monkey's uncle* — the uncle of the monkey

*horse's mouth* — the mouth of the horse

*pig's eye* — the eye of the pig

Note that even when the word ends in "s," the ending is usually " 's," since that is how we pronounce it.

*Examples*

---

*James's novels* — the novels of James

*Stevens's poetry* — the poetry of Stevens

2. **Add "s' " to the form of the possessive case if the owners are plural.**

*Examples*

---

*workers' coalition* — the coalition of workers

*boys' team* — the team of boys

But note that words that do not form the plural with "s" are made possessive by the addition of " 's."

*Examples*

---

*women's rights* — the rights of women

*people's court* — the court of people

*men's washroom* — the washroom of men

3. **Do not use an apostrophe with possessive pronouns.**

*Example*

---

*The villa is his, the Mercedes is hers, and the Swiss bank account is theirs.*

Note that "its" (another possessive pronoun) also does not have an apostrophe. Do not confuse the possessive pronoun "its" with the contraction for "it is."

## Examples

*It's time to take you home.* (It is time)

*Its diaper wet, the baby fussed noisily.* (possessive case)

## CHAPTER 16 EXERCISE A

Correct the following sentences by adding apostrophes where necessary. Turn to p. 208 for answers.

1. They went to Rodgers and Hammersteins *The King and I* and Gershwins *Porgy and Bess* as well as to more contemporary things like Jonathan Larsons *Rent* and Kander and Ebbs *Kiss of the Spider Woman*.

2. The department head compared the facultys new programs of recruitment to Tim Hortons efforts to offer bagels as well as doughnuts.

3. A bagels cost can't really compare to tuitions massive increases in a few years time, however.

4. The actors baby teeth were knocked out by the riot police; she was protesting the governments cutback of arts funding.

5. Georges pets were a dog named Trouble and a cat named Clio, after the muse of history: the dogs name was inaccurate since he was friendly and well behaved; the cats name was unsuitable since historys a blank to her.

6. Gilberts passion was garlic: the familys meal always featured its flavours; no weeks groceries were complete without it, so his friends reactions were to keep their distance.

7. Ellens office was chaotic, and she seldom returned her clients calls or paid her creditors bills: she reasoned that she was right to ignore their requests; after all, they ignored hers.

8. Scarlett was her fathers daughter: she always went straight to the horses mouth, and she thought she was the cats meow.

9. The Beatles claim to fame was their ability to influence not just musics directions, but young peoples fashions and a whole generations attitudes.

10. Company always regretted visits to the Strindbergs house because the couples arguments were so vehement, and their relatives conversations were so distressing.

## CHAPTER 16 EXERCISE B

Correct the following sentences by adding apostrophes where necessary. Answers are on p. 208.

1. After a hard days negotiations, Theos body refused to relax, and its tenseness prompted her husband to remind her of the worry dolls powers; she put them on the bureaus surface, and she soon had a pleasant nights sleep.

2. Unimpressed by the citys magnificence even from the tallest buildings outlook point, Cass responded with a yawn, captured forever in Alfreds photos of their trip.

3. Its unclear whether Denises spouses influence got her back on the job despite the cutbacks impact, but some people suspect nepotisms influence.

4. Margaret Atwoods latest novel, *Alias Grace,* is taken from historys pages: she recounts a womans story, and her responses to accusations of murder.

5. Joanne Kates restaurant column in *The Globe and Mail* has its charms: she describes all the eateries glories and flaws unflinchingly from a critics perspective.

6. Margie Gillis dancing is inspirational and energetic; its strength and beauty are well known to Canadas lovers of dance.

7. Charles Dickens novels are best in their original forms. Some film directors talents have enabled them to adapt the works into successful movies, but stage directors ambitions are usually thwarted when Victorian writers stories are turned into plays.

8. John Berendts non-fiction work *Midnight in the Garden of Good and Evil* chronicles Savannahs citizens over several years span.

9. Atom Egoyans film work in movies like *Exotica* is complemented by his contributions to the Canadian Opera Companys repertoire in a recent production of Strauss *Salome.*

10. Jane Austens fame has spread in popular cultures circles in recent years: one notable success was Emma Thompsons screenplay of *Sense and Sensibility.*

# Elements of Style: Structuring the Sentences

> Every style that is not boring is a good one.
> *Voltaire*

Variety in your sentence structure will ensure that your reader pays attention, not only to what you say, but also to the way you say it. Try to develop an awareness of the subtle changes in emphasis and reading pace that occur when you modify the structure of a sentence. Such consciousness will enhance your style and impress your reader.

## ■ Sentence Variation

**1.  Vary your sentence structure.**

The following are examples of different types of sentences.

**Simple Sentence** — one independent clause

*Donald and Ivana split their assets equitably in the divorce settlement.*

**Compound Sentence** — two independent clauses joined by one of the co-ordinating conjunctions (and, or, nor, for, but, yet, so)

*Donald kept his business empire, and Ivana kept her wardrobe and her cosmetics.*

**Complex Sentence** — one independent clause joined to one dependent clause

*Marriage is a lottery in which couples stake their happiness and their worldly goods.*

Note:  Dependent clauses begin with a subordinating conjunction, such as one of the following:

| | | | |
|---|---|---|---|
| after | because | however | that |
| although | before | if | though |
| as | how | since | |

Subordinate, or dependent, clauses also begin with words starting with a "wh–" — when, where, why, which, who, while, whereas, what — except where these words introduce questions.

**Compound-Complex Sentence** — a compound sentence joined to a complex sentence

> *They knew that a lot of people didn't expect their marriage to last, so they celebrated their first anniversary six months early.*

2. **Practise subordination by converting groups of simple or compound sentences you find in your writing into complex sentences.**

*Example*
_____

> *The patient in the clinic asked a question. Why is it that we talk to God, and we call it praying. God talks to us, and doctors call it schizophrenia.*

> REVISED: *The patient in the clinic asked why when we talk to God, we call it praying, whereas when God talks to us, doctors call it schizophrenia.*

3. **Practise joining simple sentences together using verbal phrases rather than subordinators. Start by changing the verb into a participle (usually ending in "ing" or "ed"). Then remove its subject, and connect it to the appropriate word in the following sentence.**

*Example*
_____

> *Joshua stayed in bed this morning. He is suffering from a hangover.*

> REVISED: *Suffering from a hangover, Joshua stayed in bed this morning.*

4. **Practise cutting tangled constructions down to size by using simple sentences where the reader might have difficulty in understanding or where you wish to place more emphasis.**

*Example*
_____

> *A factory job is superior to a job requiring post-secondary education. Some would argue the opposite. Still, the advantages of a factory job are numerous. Here are some of these advantages. A factory worker makes more money at an earlier age than a college student. Thus he can live on his own earlier. A factory worker also has more spare time to pursue other goals. There is also less stress placed on a factory worker. He is more likely to be happy and healthy.*

> REVISED: *Although some would argue the opposite, a factory job is superior to a job requiring post-secondary education. Because a factory worker makes more money at an earlier age than a college student, he is able to live on his own earlier. In addition, because a factory worker has more time to pursue other goals and faces less stress than someone in a white-collar job, he is more likely to be happy and healthy.*

5. **Try converting some of the phrases and dependent clauses in your writing into absolutes (phrases with connecting words removed). Keep the subject of the clause and its accompanying participle; remove other words.**

*Example*

---

*Because his tire was flat and his hopes of winning races were gone, Mario decided to become a gas-station attendant.*

REVISED: *His tire flat and his hopes of winning races gone, Mario decided to become a gas-station attendant.*

6.  **Vary your sentences by making them more suspenseful. The typical English sentence moves directly from subject to verb to object or complement, a structure often called "loose." In other languages, the word order is often not so direct, placing subject or verb near the end of the sentence. This structure is called "periodic." Try making your own sentences periodic occasionally, so that the impact of the thought is delayed.**

*Examples*

---

LOOSE: *Desmond gave Molly a diamond ring.*

PERIODIC: *Shyly, anxiously, and with tears in his eyes, Desmond gave Molly a diamond ring.*

---

## CHAPTER 17 EXERCISES

1.  Join these sentences, using verbal phrases. Answers are on p. 209.

    a.  Sadie wanted to catch her canary. She chased it around the room with a guppy net, but the bird eluded her.
    b.  Stacey wished to keep things neat and organized. She insisted that doors and windows be kept shut both at work and at home. She folded plastic bags neatly into small squares before she put them away.
    c.  Steve relished his position as hall monitor. He walked through the school corridors with the confidence and attitude of a rooster, and boasted that his employment even improved his golf game.

2.  Rewrite these sentences, using absolutes, rather than dependent clauses or simple sentences.

    a.  Salvador was lonely and bored. He put an ad in the personals column.
    b.  The ad was a disaster. It attracted only other lonely, bored people, not socially adjusted ones.
    c.  When he ended the phone call, Salvador sadly reported that it wasn't his dream date, but a social worker, asking if he had received his welfare cheque.

3.  Rewrite these simple sentences to form complex sentences.

    a.  Gio and Millard tried to resist the temptation to buy a dog. They found Manfred, a gorgeous golden Labrador retriever, and bought him despite their misgivings.
    b.  Matilda swore off licorice. It stuck to her teeth and made her feel sick afterwards.
    c.  The nurse encouraged her patient. To coax him along, she always sang "Raindrops Keep Fallin' On My Head."

4. Take the following loose sentences and make them periodic. Make the subject or the verb more complicated, or change the word order to delay the impact of the sentence.

   a. Her necklace was found on the floor behind a heavy piece of furniture.
   b. They missed the plane, though Cecily and Sedgwick ran through the airport in a frenzy.
   c. Children are increasingly becoming perpetrators of crime.

5. Analyze an essay that you have recently written, or are writing, to determine what sentence patterns you use most commonly. Rewrite some of the sentences, and examine the changes in emphasis that such revision creates.

6. Analyze some writing by an author you admire. Try to model some sentences on the structure of those you find.

## Parallelism

Parallelism is one of the basic components of good writing style. The repetitive rhythm of parallel structure allows the reader to anticipate what comes next and to keep the overall construction in mind. Consider the following sentences:

> NOT PARALLEL: *Dawn finished her essay by staying up all night, working without a break, and finally, she asked her mother to type the paper for her.*

> PARALLEL: *Dawn finished her essay by staying up all night, working without a break, and finally, asking her mother to type the paper for her.*

Making sentences that are logical, powerful, and easy to understand requires a developed sense of parallel construction. To sharpen this sense, you need to become aware of certain basic requirements of balanced sentence structure.

### 1. Make sure grammatical elements match.

To form a parallel construction, join nouns with nouns, verbs with verbs, participles with participles, adjectives with adjectives, and so on. Connecting words like "and," "or," "but," "yet" are often signals of the need for a parallel construction.

> NOT PARALLEL: *The actor was handsome, articulate, and he loved to look at himself in a mirror.*

> PARALLEL: *The actor was handsome, articulate, and vain, loving to look at himself in a mirror.*

Since the first two items are adjectives ("handsome" and "articulate"), the last item in the series should be an adjective too.

> NOT PARALLEL: *People who are in debt should give up credit cards, borrowing money, eating out in expensive restaurants, and living above their means.*

> PARALLEL: *People who are in debt should give up using credit cards, borrowing money, eating out in expensive restaurants, and living above their means.*

The parallelism is improved when each of the nouns in question is preceded by an "ing" form.

NOT PARALLEL: *They divorced because the husband thought that no one should read while he was talking, and the wife thought that while she was reading, no one should talk.*

PARALLEL: *They divorced because the husband thought that no one should read while he was talking, and the wife thought that no one should talk while she was reading.*

The balance is improved by maintaining the same word order in each clause.

## 2. Use parallel constructions after "than" or "as."

NOT PARALLEL: *It is better to light a candle than curse the darkness.*

PARALLEL: *It is better to light a candle than to curse the darkness.*

What follows "than" should be parallel with what precedes. Hence, the word "to" should be repeated.

NOT PARALLEL: *My grades are just as good as Stephanie.*

PARALLEL: *My grades are just as good as Stephanie's.*

OR: *My grades are just as good as Stephanie's grades are.*

The grades are being compared, not the grades and Stephanie.

## 3. Balance sentence elements connected by correlatives.

Correlatives come in pairs. They include "not only . . . but also," "both . . . and," "either . . . or," "neither . . . nor," "whether . . . or."

The grammatical constructions that follow the first co-ordinator should also follow the second.

NOT PARALLEL: *Derek didn't only apologize to her and admit that he had been wrong, he gave her a red rose and asked her forgiveness.*

PARALLEL: *Not only did Derek apologize to her and admit that he had been wrong, but he also gave her a red rose and asked her forgiveness.*

Correlative conjunctions are used here to join two clauses.

NOT PARALLEL: *Whether you take the bus or if you go by plane, two days is not long enough for a trip to Disneyland.*

PARALLEL: *Whether you take the bus or you go by plane, two days is not long enough for a trip to Disneyland.*

Correlatives are used here to join two main clauses. Note the revisions in the following sentences:

NOT PARALLEL: *Arnold was sound both mentally and in body.*

PARALLEL: *Arnold was sound both in mind and in body.*

What follows "both" should be grammatically parallel to what follows "and."

NOT PARALLEL: *You either give Jason his toy back, or I'll tell your mother.*

PARALLEL: *Either you give Jason his toy back, or I'll tell your mother.*

What follows "either" must be grammatically parallel to what follows "or." In this case, a subject and verb follow both items.

4. **Parallel constructions may also be indicated by transitional signposts such as "first," "second," and "third."**

   NOT PARALLEL: *The sales clerk quit his job: first, the customers were rude; second, he was tired of minimum wage; and third, disgusted at having to work on Saturday nights.*

   PARALLEL: *The sales clerk quit his job: first, the customers were rude; second, he was tired of minimum wage; and third, he was disgusted at having to work on Saturday nights.*

5. **Make sure that items in a list are grammatically parallel.**

   NOT PARALLEL: *This report makes four recommendations:*
   *1. divers should be certified by an accredited school*
   *2. they should wear appropriate equipment at all times*
   *3. they should work in pairs*
   *4. regular health checkups*

   PARALLEL: *This report makes four recommendations:*
   *1. divers should be certified by an accredited school*
   *2. they should wear appropriate equipment at all times*
   *3. they should work in pairs*
   *4. they should get regular health checkups*

In this case, the items listed have been changed so that they are all main clauses; in the incorrect example, the fourth item is a phrase.

Remember that parallel construction need not be confined to words and phrases; it may extend to subordinate clauses and to sentences. Effective use of parallel structure will enhance your writing by making it clear, balanced, and carefully structured.

   NOT PARALLEL: *Every one of these buildings, public and private, restored or dilapidated, will share a similar fate: bought by a developer, or if the city expands, they will be destroyed.*

   PARALLEL: *Every one of these buildings, public and private, restored or dilapidated, will share a similar fate: if a developer buys them, or if the city expands, they will be destroyed.*

"Or" in the corrected sentence joins two subordinate clauses both in the active voice.

---

## CHAPTER 17 EXERCISE A

Correct any faulty parallelism you find in the following sentences. Check your answers on p. 210.

1. Bernice went into hospital, received flowers and other tokens of affection, and she enjoyed her physical complaints immensely.

2. Go to Hawaii for two weeks, or you will suffer unbearable jet lag after only a short stay.

3. On their visit to Vancouver, the twins went to Stanley Park, the art gallery, and took in a performance of "Bard on the Beach."

4. Being sound mentally and in body is essential when you make a legal document.

5. Evelyn not only sent greeting cards to her brothers and sisters, but also she made sure they were given some of her famous homemade pies.

6. When reviewing a restaurant, you have to be mindful of service, ambience, and whether the food is any good.

7. To get an MBA, you need lots of money to cover the high cost of tuition, experience or expertise in business, and it wouldn't hurt to have great reserves of stamina.

8. Jane put on her long red gown, looked at herself hesitantly in the mirror, and then she remembered that she wanted to rent the video *Attack of the Killer Tomatoes!*

9. Mala missed her bus, spilled coffee all over herself, and she vowed she would complain to the transit company.

10. Carlos loved Paris even though he suffered in its heat, could barely afford to buy a baguette, and he lost ten pounds carrying his baggage.

## CHAPTER 17 EXERCISE B

Correct any faulty parallelism you find in the following sentences. Answers are on p. 210.

1. Edith and Henry waved at the tourists sailing by on the river, they enjoyed the scenery and chuckled to think that they would appear in people's home movies.

2. Kevin had an exhilarating swim, realized he couldn't find his clothes, and then he spent hours wandering the beach in the nude, wishing he had worn sunscreen.

3. Not only did Nellie and Daphne disagree about the colour of the carpet, but also about the placement of the paintings.

4. The therapist calmed Hugo's fears, made several suggestions, he recorded a tape, and then asked for a credit card number.

5. Colm either learns some manners on the telephone, or he will have to step down from his position in the department.

6. You either could let Peggy and her basset hound into the living room, or you could go out on the front porch to chat.

7. Iain's job was as precarious as Rob.

8. Neither the cabbage rolls and rice nor did the borscht please Rex.

9. Emilio received a fur hat for his birthday, tried it on, and he immediately began to imitate Bucky Beaver.

10. Accusations of favouritism will neither offend me, nor will they stop me from hiring my friends.

# ■ Active and Passive Voice

The voice of a verb tells you whether the subject acts or is acted upon. There are two voices: active and passive. In the active voice, the sentence takes this form: actor, verb, receiver. In the passive voice, the form is inverted: receiver, verb, actor, and the verb always includes some form of "to be."

In an active sentence, the subject is the actor:

*The zookeeper fed the lion raw meat.*

In a passive sentence, the subject is acted upon:

*The raw meat was fed to the lion by the zookeeper.*

Keep these points in mind when you decide which voice is more appropriate in a given context:

1. **The active voice is more forthright and usually more concise.**
2. **The active voice emphasizes the actor; the passive voice emphasizes the receiver of an action. In the example above, the zookeeper is the subject in the active sample; the raw meat is the subject in the passive sample.**
3. **The active voice emphasizes action; the passive is best used to describe stasis.**

   ACTIVE: *The pit bull terrier bit the postman.*

   PASSIVE: *The postman was bitten by the pit bull terrier.*

4. **The passive voice is awkward when it is used to avoid direct phrasing or when it results in unclear, lengthy constructions.**

   ACTIVE: *Amos, the shifty used car dealer, sold fifty lemons last month.* (direct)

   PASSIVE: *Last month, fifty lemons were sold.* (indirect: this rather dishonest use of the passive voice is typical of writers who wish to avoid responsibility for something or who wish to keep things impersonal)

   ACTIVE: *At Hallowe'en, Harry played a prank on his mother.* (clear)

   PASSIVE: *At Hallowe'en, a prank was played on his mother by Harry.* (unclear and lengthy)

5. **The passive voice is occasionally useful to avoid overuse of the pronoun "I." Be wary of overuse of the passive voice, however.**

   ACTIVE: *I based this study on interviews with computer operators across the country.*

   PASSIVE: *This study is based on interviews with computer operators across the country.*

6. **Remember that the passive voice is useful when you wish to emphasize the receiver of the action, rather than the performer.**

   ACTIVE: *The spectators could see the fireworks for miles.*

   PASSIVE: *The fireworks could be seen for miles.*

Since it is unimportant who could see the fireworks, the passive is preferable here.

7. **The passive voice is also the best choice when you wish to avoid being too personal.**

ACTIVE: *You must obey this summons immediately.*

PASSIVE: *This summons must be obeyed immediately.*

Since the summons is meant to be formal and impersonal, the passive is preferable here.

## CHAPTER 17 EXERCISE A

Identify all the verbs in the following sentences as active or passive. Discuss which you would change and why. Answers are on p. 211.

1. Beaufort's interest in jigsaw puzzles was spurred on by his mother who hoped he would be entertained on his next long train journey.

2. At the family picnic, hamburgers were eaten even though Evelina was said to have stocked up on steaks to be fed to her Dobermans afterwards.

3. Raw onions were adored by Gustave though fellow workers were not enamoured of his persistent odour.

4. Avery's new bifocals were purchased at a discount optician; he was forced by constant reading problems to get them, but he was nevertheless revolted at this sign of his impending old age.

5. City streets were shovelled promptly after a number of complaints were received from concerned citizens who had been inconvenienced.

6. Consumers were bombarded with glossy ads encouraging them to buy new electronic equipment during the holiday season, and although stores were well stocked, buyers were not sufficiently impressed.

7. It was decided by the university that some washrooms should be closed, some tuitions should be doubled, and most cleaning staff should be laid off.

8. Although tobacco's ill effects are well documented, increase in its use among teenage girls has been shown.

9. Ann Marie MacDonald's work *Good Night Desdemona, Good Morning Juliet* has been well received by audiences and critics. She sets her play partly inside two of Shakespeare's plays and partly in a contemporary graduate school.

10. *Sled* and *White Biting Dog* were both written by Judith Thompson.

## CHAPTER 17 EXERCISE B

Identify all the verbs in the following sentences as active or passive. Discuss which you would change and why. Check your answers on p. 211.

1. The notebook computer was stolen by someone in the bus station after the unwary executive left it by the pay phone.

2. Flights were cancelled and motorists were stranded by a freak snowstorm that hit Canada's west coast.

3. Céline Dion's records sold well internationally, as did Alanis Morissette's; the Canadian music industry has benefited tremendously from their triumphs.

4. Gary Larsen's cartoons will be missed now that he no longer writes *The Far Side*.

5. You will be fired if your attitude is not improved by next week, Dilbert.

6. Unemployment has been renamed by the media "involuntary leisure time."

7. Students' papers were allegedly collected, thrown down a flight of stairs, and then graded by the disgruntled instructor, according to the height or depth the papers reached.

8. The plaque was mounted on the wall to prevent vandalism; unfortunately, if the plaque were later judged better placed somewhere else, the wall would have to be removed.

9. Fatima's vehicle was badly damaged by the accident; she lost control, and her car rolled into the ditch, but luckily, she was uninjured by the impact.

10. The open house was well attended: all the guests were wined and dined by the sponsors, and timeshares were offered to them for sale.

# Reducing Wordiness

> Oh, shun, lad, the life of an author.
>   It's nothing but worry and waste.
> Avoid that utensil,
> The labouring pencil,
>   And pick up the scissors and paste.
> *Phyllis McGinley*

A wordy essay does not necessarily transgress the word limit of the assignment. Rather, it contains extraneous words that contribute nothing to the meaning and drain force from the essay's argument.

Wordy writing is often characteristic of a first draft. It is close to idle chat: though spontaneous and sometimes even fascinating, it lacks direction. It wanders, perhaps arriving eventually at meaning; it does not set out in orderly pursuit of it. A wordy essay is often a sign of poorly revised and overdressed thought.

Make every word fit. If you can make your writing more succinct, your work will be clearer, and your reader will be more attentive. A few suggestions for improving the conciseness of your writing are listed below.

## ■ A Perfect Fit

### Avoid visible seams

When talking, we commonly join ideas together randomly. Speed is the goal, not beautiful construction. Consider the following example:

### *Example*

*Emilio bought the book.*

You decide to add a further detail.

*Emilio bought the book, which was reputed to be steamy and sensational.*

Your new thought shows an obvious seam. "Which" and "that" can often be removed to produce a more graceful line.

*Emilio bought the book, reputed to be steamy and sensational.*

## Avoid frills

Often, a speaker describes something by using words accompanied by adverbs meant to accentuate their effect. Here are some examples:

| | |
|---|---|
| ✗ quite elegant | ✗ extremely upset |
| ✗ very angry | ✗ altogether pleased |
| ✗ rather uneasy | ✗ not true |

Replace these with stronger, less wordy, expressions:

| | |
|---|---|
| ✓ splendid | ✓ distraught |
| ✓ irate | ✓ ecstatic |
| ✓ anxious | ✓ false |

In writing, the search for impact is better served by a stronger word, rather than a modified word. And, in writing, there is time to search for it. Use that time to dress your thoughts appropriately.

The same advice holds true for redundant wording. Avoid phrases like these:

| | |
|---|---|
| ✗ past history | ✓ history |
| ✗ triangular in shape | ✓ triangular |
| ✗ the city of Saskatoon | ✓ Saskatoon |
| ✗ personal opinion | ✓ opinion |
| ✗ refer back | ✓ refer |
| ✗ exactly identical | ✓ identical |

In each case, the omitted words added nothing to the meaning.

## Avoid baggy constructions

A baggy sentence often contains vague words intended to conceal vague thoughts. Such sentences invariably include the following all-too-common words and phrases. Some of these can be excised. Most can be replaced by a single word.

| | |
|---|---|
| ✗ due to the fact that | ✓ because |
| ✗ during the time that | ✓ when |
| ✗ with regard to | ✓ about |
| ✗ being | (omit) |
| ✗ previous to | ✓ before |
| ✗ at which time | ✓ when |
| ✗ in the very near future | ✓ soon |
| ✗ in the event that | ✓ if |

Tentative language and unnecessary compound verbs are another frequent cause of bagginess. Avoid phrases like the following:

| | |
|---|---|
| ✗ make assumptions about | ✗ be in a position to |
| ✗ come to the conclusion | ✗ make a recommendation |
| ✗ exhibit a tendency to | ✗ take action on |

Substitute:

| | |
|---|---|
| ✓ assume | ✓ can |
| ✓ conclude | ✓ recommend |
| ✓ tend | ✓ act |

## Avoid the "grand style"

Writing in the "grand style" uses pompous phrasing to clothe humble ideas. Pompous introductions are a common source of the problem:

✗ *It is this theory which needs . . .*
✓ *This theory needs . . .*

✗ *It was his view that . . .*
✓ *He thought that . . .*

## Avoid excessive formality

Just as you wouldn't wear evening dress to compete in a bowling tournament, so you should not use static language to describe active thoughts.

Where possible, keep sentences in their typical order — use the active voice, and move from subject to verb to object. "The Prime Minister gave the order" is a much more direct statement than the passive construction "The order was given by the Prime Minister."

✗ *A decision was made by the committee to conduct further studies.*
✓ *The committee decided to conduct further studies.*

While the passive mode has its uses (as discussed earlier), it *is* wordier, less forceful, and generally harder to understand. It is all talk and no action. When revising, keep a watchful eye on the number of times you resort to the static passive voice. It can occasionally serve as a tactful way of avoiding direct confrontation.

### *Example*

*PASSIVE: This amount is owing.* (what the bill says)

*ACTIVE: You owe us this amount.* (what the bill means)

# ■ Wordiness Analyzed

The preceding examples illustrate that wordiness is most often caused by speech habits not entirely abandoned in writing. To analyze the causes of your own wordiness, note especially any words you use to *warm up* as you begin to write, to *cover up* your insecurities and uncertainties as you proceed, or to *spruce up* a thought better left unadorned.

# ■ Preventive Measures

When editing, check to see that your sentences are designed for simplicity, concreteness, action, grace, and impact.

---

### CHAPTER 18 EXERCISE

Improve the following sentences by removing or changing redundant words or phrases. Answers are on p. 212.

1. At this point in time, Ralph usually opts to ride his bike to his place of employment, but he keeps his van running in order to transport his musical instruments from place to place.

2. The necessity of using electronic mail made an impression on Kay, though she still had a preference for remaining in close physical proximity to those for whom she had love and affection.

3. Sandra, in my own personal estimate, is not a capable hairdresser, and it will be essential for me to seek someone out to replace her in that capacity.

4. Piglet reported to Winnie that the balloon which had broken was small in size and red in colour.

5. Cecil's exhibition at the art gallery used household furniture for the purpose of exploring the gradual loss and decline of domestic values in the family; I am not in a position to judge whether the work is of an innovative nature or not.

6. Steve had a plan to immortalize the story of his roommates: he was of the opinion that the story of Bobby, Luciano, and Bruce would be an entertaining situation comedy, although he had some doubt about whether or not it would be believable to viewers.

7. It is this print which was purchased at the mall after Carmelina haggled with the salesclerk over considerations of its price.

8. The fact that we find ourselves unable to appreciate the jokes that he tells is of no importance due to the simple reason that we are responsible for making the invitation to him; it is we who must be tolerant of his presence.

9. Being a woman who was married and who planned to give birth to children, Fiona had made the decision to take her husband's last name.

10. Students who wish to attain high marks have a tendency to forget that teachers who are overworked might give their consent if they received more co-operation.

# PART SEVEN

# Reviewing the Results

# Perfecting the Essay

If critics want to help me, let them come sit next
to me while I'm writing.

*Rita Mae Brown*

The revision process involves more than fussing over a few typographical errors; it should ideally be a process that reconceives and reviews the entire essay: not only its mechanics, but its structure and its thought. While it is usually valuable to proceed as this book recommends — from thesis to outline, to research (if required), to first draft — the first written draft you produce is unlikely to be the clearest version of your thinking on any given subject. Bearing in mind your own shortcomings as a writer, as you have come to know them in your writing experience, prepare yourself to judge your own work in its entirety. Much of your real writing will be done at this stage, now that you are free to put yourself in the reader's position and imagine your paper's impact on him or her.

Remember that an essay has a duty to be unified, clear, and coherent. Accordingly, judge your work by the relevance of the information you have provided, by its ability to explain itself fully and clearly, and by its ability to make connections in the reader's mind. Putting yourself in the reader's position means that you must re-examine your assumptions about the subject matter and the reader's knowledge of it, and you must be willing to query the things that strike you as doubtful or awkward as you read. Detachment is crucial here, as is the time to do a good job.

Even after all your hard work, some minor but significant detail may affect the reader's perception of your paper. Often these errors are the most embarrassing ones, errors that undercut your effort and distract the reader's attention from the elegance of your essay's form and the substance of its content. Like the emperor with no clothes, you and your work may be easily subjected to ridicule or to charges of arrogance if you neglect responsible proofreading and stringent self-criticism. To ensure the quality of your work, follow these steps:

## 1. Move from the whole to the parts.

Revising is complicated. The process involves more than superficial corrections of mechanical errors. It involves a careful reconsideration of every part of your draft. Try to follow this sequence, or one adapted to suit you, when you revise your papers.

a. Check your facts. Does anything need to be added or changed?
b. Rethink your scheme of organization. Does the order make sense?
c. Test paragraph structure. Are your ideas developed and linked properly?
d. Read over your sentences. Are they clear, smooth, varied?
e. Examine your word choice. Is it accurate, suitable, effective?
f. Check your grammar and spelling. Is the paper free of errors?

## 2. Reflect on your image.

Just as you wouldn't buy an item of clothing without first looking to see if it suited you and fit properly, don't write a paper and then submit it without first assessing its immediate impact on its readers. Reread the paper, scrutinizing its details very carefully — preferably a few days after you have written it. Reading aloud will help you find any awkward instances of grammatical construction and style. If you *still* feel insecure, ask a friend to read it too.

## 3. If you can't be perfect, be careful.

Some errors, in this imperfect world, may still creep in. Make necessary corrections as unobtrusively as possible. Resist the impulse to retype the whole paper (possibly introducing new errors) and instead make the corrections neatly in black ink — above the line. Stroke out unwanted letters with a small vertical line, and remove repeated words by the judicious use of "white-out" (liquid paper) or the simple horizontal stroke of a pen.

## 4. Make your paper "easy on the eyes."

Don't allow your essay to offend the eye. Specifically, avoid erasable bond paper (which baffles the instructor who tries to write on it). Avoid typewriter ribbon so faded that you develop eyestrain trying to read a paper typed with it. Make your handwriting bold, large, and neat. If you submit a computer printout, take special care in proofreading to avoid errors that may have been introduced in production. Submit the paper in a tidy folder, neatly stapled or paper-clipped (as your instructor may prefer). Even if neatness is not an acknowledged criterion of excellence, there is no question that first impressions have a lasting effect.

## 5. Tie up any loose threads.

Don't submit your paper without checking such details as page numbers, exact quotations, bibliographical information, doubtful spellings, word divisions, and grammatical constructions.

## 6. Follow the "dress code."

Make sure that your assignment adheres to any conditions explicitly stated by the instructor, however arbitrary or trivial such matters may seem to you. Check to see that the mechanical format of your paper conforms to the expected standards of the instructor. Such items as the treatment of abbreviations, bibliographical arrangement, even the format of the title page and the position and form of page numbers need careful attention. Although you may have already invested considerable time in these matters, a last-minute check is a good idea.

# Mending the Essay

> Writing is pretty crummy on the nerves.
>
> *Paul Theroux*

If, when you get an essay back, you find that your work has been disappointing, there are still some things you can do to redeem yourself. It may be too late to get the kind of grade that you had in mind on this particular paper, but some of the tactics proposed below ought to make the next essay better.

First, don't throw the paper away in a fit of glee or gloom. You write essays not only to get grades but also to learn how to write. Long after you have forgotten the facts and figures involved in writing your paper, you will still have the writing skills that were developed in its preparation. Your reading, writing, and research skills are the most visible parts of your education long after you graduate.

## ◼ Deciphering Comments

### 1. Read the grader's comments when your essays are returned to you — regardless of the grade you receive.

Don't read only the comments accompanying the grade at the end of the paper, but also any questions or hints dropped in the margins or within the text of the paper.

### 2. Next, see that you understand what the comments and questions mean.

The list below should help:

| | |
|---|---|
| *agr* | — *error in agreement (subject/verb or antecedent/pronoun)* |
| *awk* | — *awkward wording* |
| *case* | — *error in pronoun case* |
| *cs* | — *comma splice* |
| *D* | — *problem with diction* |
| *dm* | — *dangling modifier* |
| *doc* | — *error in documentation* |
| *frag* | — *sentence fragment* |
| *gr* | — *error in grammar or usage* |
| *mm* | — *misplaced modifier* |
| *p* | — *error in punctuation* |
| *par* | — *problem with paragraphing* |
| *pass* | — *overuse of the passive voice* |
| *ref* | — *problem with pronoun reference* |
| *rep* | — *repetition* |

| run-on | — run-on sentence |
| shift | — shift in verb tense or logic |
| sp | — error in spelling |
| T | — error in verb tense |
| TS | — problem with thesis statement |
| trans | — transition |
| ‖ | — faulty parallelism |
| ∧ | — something missing |
| wdy | — problem with wordiness |

3. **Ask your instructor to explain a particular comment, if you do not understand it.**

4. **When you have read through the comments, try to analyze the kind of mistakes that you make most frequently and determine that you will take steps to eliminate them.**

5. **Next, consult a reliable guide in order to correct your mistakes.**

Such guides include a dictionary (for spelling errors and errors of usage), a writing/grammar handbook (such as this one), or a guide to proper format of notes and bibliography (such as the *MLA Handbook*).

## ■ Learning from Experience

### 1. Analyze the strengths and weaknesses of your style.

At first, this may seem a puzzling endeavour, but after a time you should be able to discern changes in your writing — not only in its mechanics, but in the development of its thought as well.

### 2. Analyze your writing habits.

Do you find that you have certain favourite expressions that crop up too often? Do your readers frequently comment that your sentences are too complex or too simple? Do certain tactics in your argument often meet with an unfavourable response? Paying attention to these trends in your collected essays will enable you to become more sensitive to your patterns of self-expression and more able to prevent problems in the future.

### 3. Keep a list of your most common spelling and grammar errors from past work.

Refer to this list when you are about to write the final draft of your next paper. It may help eliminate some pitfalls.

### 4. Exercise your writing skills.

Reading is probably not a strong enough remedy to cure you of some errors; writing is the recommended therapy. If possible, set yourself the task of completing some exercises aimed at a specific problem diagnosed by your instructor. If, for example, dangling modifiers are a persistent problem, consult the section in this book on their diagnosis and treatment. Your instructor may agree to check your answers afterwards.

### 5. Rewrite.

Rewriting is also a good way of curing some of the ills of essay writing. Try, for example, to recast a troublesome paragraph in clearer, smoother prose, incorporating your instructor's suggestions. Remember, though, that no writer ever developed a style mechanically; it is intimately related to thought. Rethink your thoughts as you rewrite. You will learn a great deal about the impact your writing has on its readers if you remember the grader's comments.

### 6. Work through appropriate sections of this book with an essay that has just been returned.

This exercise will help you in your next essay assignment.

### 7. Experiment.

Writing should not always be a chore. Sometimes, when you find yourself able to express something exactly the way you want to, writing becomes play. Allow yourself to become comfortable as you write. Remember that your real writing purpose, grades and completed assignments aside, is to say what you want to say. Practice will make writing a satisfying form of self-expression.

# Glossary of Usage

I can't write five words but that I change seven.
*Dorothy Parker*

This glossary lists some words that are a common source of errors, either because they are confused with other words, or because they are not acceptable in standard usage. Check through this list if you are in doubt about a particular usage.

**accept/except**
"Accept" is a verb that means to "consent to"; "except" is a verb or a preposition that means "to exclude."

*I would **accept** your proposition **except** for my husband and six children.*

**advice/advise**
"Advice" is a noun; "advise" is a verb.

*I **advise** you to follow your mother's **advice**.*

**affect/effect**
"Affect" is usually a verb; "effect" is usually a noun. Note, however, that "effect" may occasionally be a verb, meaning "to bring about."

*His break-up with his girlfriend **affected** his grade point average.*
*A broken heart may have a bad **effect** on scholastic achievement.*
*He thought that by writing a tear-stained letter he could perhaps **effect** a reconciliation.*

**allude/elude**
"To allude" means "to make indirect reference to"; "to elude" means "to escape."

*A lewd reference may **elude** you, but it may perhaps **allude** to another literary source.*

**allusion/illusion**
The first is a veiled or indirect reference; the second is a deception.

*She found the poet's **allusion** to Shakespeare; her belief that the words came from Milton was an **illusion**.*

**a lot/allot**
"A lot" is a colloquialism for "many" or "a great deal"; "to allot" is a verb, meaning "to divide" or "to parcel out." There is no form "alot."

*Each of the heiresses had been **allotted a lot** of their grandfather's fortune.*

## all together/altogether

The first means "in a group"; the second means "completely" or "entirely."

**All together**, *the students in the class decided that the teacher was* **altogether** *incompetent.*

## all right/alright

The *first* is the correct spelling.

## among/between

"Among" involves more than two; "between" involves just two.

**Among** *his peers he is considered a genius;* **between** *you and me, I think he is overrated.*

## amount of/number of

"Amount of" is for quantities that cannot be counted and hence is followed by a singular noun; "a number of" is for quantities that may be counted and takes a plural noun.

*A* **number** *of students drink a large* **amount** *of alcohol.*

## as/because

"Because" should be used instead of "as" in a sentence meant to show cause and effect, since "as" or "while" may also refer to the passage of time.

✗ **As** *he was awaiting trial, he refused to speak to the press.* (ambiguous)
✓ **Because** *he was awaiting trial, he refused to speak to the press.*

## aspect

Avoid this vague word. While not always incorrect, it often contributes to vagueness.

## being/being as/being that

"Being" can almost always be eliminated. "Being as" or "being that" should be replaced by "because" or "since."

## bottom line

This popular bit of financial jargon has no place in formal writing.

## can/may

"Can" implies ability; "may" implies permission or possibility.

*I* **may** *go shopping today since I* **can** *buy anything I want.*

## in the case of

A wordy construction, best avoided.

✗ *In the* **case** *of your mother-in-law, she means well.*
✓ *Your mother-in-law means well.*

## centre on/revolve around

Avoid "centre around," an illogical phrase.

### comprises/comprised of

"Comprises" means "consists of." Do *not* use "is comprised of."

> ✗ Canada is **comprised of** ten provinces and two territories.
> ✓ Canada **comprises** ten provinces and two territories.

### conscious/conscience

"Conscious" is an adjective meaning "aware"; "conscience" is one's inner sense of morality.

> The jury became increasingly **conscious** of the criminal's lack of **conscience**.

### continual/continuous

"continual" means "repeated"; "continuous" means "without ceasing."

> Her homework was **continually** interrupted by telephone calls from vacuum cleaner salesmen.
> The air conditioner was used **continuously** throughout the long, hot day.

### could of/should of/would of

You mean "could have," "should have," "would have."

### data/criteria/phenomena/media

All of these words are plural. Their singular forms are "datum," "criterion," "phenomenon," and "medium." Check the subject and verb agreement carefully with each.

> Some people think the media **are** responsible for all modern ills.

### disinterested/uninterested

"Disinterested" means "impartial"; "uninterested" means "bored" or "unconcerned."

> The ideal referee is **disinterested** in the outcome of the game, but shouldn't be **uninterested** in the actions of the players.

### due to

"Due to" is acceptable only after some form of the verb "to be." Use "because of" to imply a causal relationship.

> The bus is **due to** arrive in fifteen minutes.
> Because of his allergies, he had to give up Muffy, his Persian cat.

### elicit/illicit

"To elicit" is a verb meaning "to evoke"; "illicit" is an adjective meaning "illegal."

> The questions at the press conference should **elicit** some response to the president's **illicit** behaviour.

### enthuse/enthused

Avoid these words. Use "enthusiastic" instead.

> Bruce Springsteen's fans were **enthusiastic** about his concert tour.

**equally as**

Do not use "equally" and "as" together. Instead, use one or the other.

> *She and her brother are* **equally** *good at contact sports.*
> *She is as good* **as** *her brother at contact sports.*

**etc.**

Avoid this abbreviation, which usually means that the author does not know what else to say.

**the fact that**

Avoid this wordy expression.

**factor**

This word generally adds nothing; leave it out.

**farther/further**

"Farther" refers to actual distance; "further" is abstract.

> *The* **farther** *he walked, the more his feet hurt.*
> *She would not stand for any* **further** *shenanigans.*

**fewer/less**

"Fewer" is used with plural nouns; "less" is used with singular nouns.

> *The* **fewer** *the guests, the* **less** *liquor we will need.*

**firstly, secondly,**

"First" and "second" are all you really need.

**hopefully**

Replace this word with "It is hoped that," or more simply, I (we) hope that.

> ✗ **Hopefully,** *the paper will be finished tomorrow.*

This sentence implies that the paper itself is hopeful.

> ✓ **It is hoped that** *the paper will be finished tomorrow.*
> ✓ **I hope** *that the paper will be finished tomorrow.*

**impact on**

"Impact" is a noun, not a verb. Replace it with "have an impact on."

> *The economy will* **have an impact on** *workers' salaries.*

**imply/infer**

"To imply" means "to suggest"; "to infer" means "to conclude."

> *She* **implied** *that he was cheap; he* **inferred** *that he should have offered to pay her bus fare.*

**input**

Avoid this word and other computer jargon, except when you are discussing computers.

**into**

Avoid using this preposition to mean "interested in."

> ✗ He was **into** macramé.
> ✓ He was **interested in** macramé.

**irregardless**

The correct word is "regardless."

**its/it's**

"Its" is the possessive form, like "his" or "her."
"It's" is a contraction for "it is" or "it has."

> That dog's bark is worse than **its** bite.
> **It's** certainly got big teeth, though.

**-ize**

Avoid some of the newly created verbs with this ending. They are part of the growing and deplorable tendency to turn nouns into verbs, as in "prioritize." There is usually a simpler form.

> ✗ He **utilized** the facilities.
> ✓ He **used** the facilities.

**lay/lie**

"Lay" takes an object; "lie" does not.

> The farmer made the hen **lie** on the nest to **lay** an egg.

**like/as/as if**

"Like" is a preposition and should not be used as a conjunction. Substitute "as" or "as if" if a clause follows.

> ✗ He looks **like** he's going to die.
> ✓ He looks **as if** he's going to die.
> ✓ He looks **like** death warmed over.

**myself**

"Myself" is not a more polite form of "I" or "me." It should be reserved for use as an intensifier or reflexive.

> ✗ The hostess introduced my wife and **myself** to the guests.
> ✓ The hostess introduced my wife and **me** to the guests.
> ✓ I, **myself**, solved the problem.
> ✓ I drove **myself** to the airport.

**parameters/perimeters**

Use "perimeters" to mean "boundaries," or to refer to a length or distance. Avoid the use of "parameters" except in its specific application to geometry.

**parent**

Do not use this word as a verb; "parenting" is also suspect. "Parenthood" is a perfectly acceptable substitute.

## practice/practise

"Practice" is the noun; "practise" is the verb.

*I know* **practice** *makes perfect, but I hate to* **practise**.

## presently

Substitute "currently" or "now." "Presently" actually means "soon."

## principal/principle

The first means "chief" or "main" as an adjective, the head of a school as a noun; the second means "a basic truth."

*His* **principal** *objection to her comments was that they were based on questionable* **principles**.

## quote/quotation

"Quote" is a verb, *not* a noun — "quotation" is the noun.

✗ *This* **quote** *from Richard Nixon makes the point clear.*
✓ *This* **quotation** *from Richard Nixon makes the point clear.*

## relate to

Use this verb to indicate how one idea is related to another. Do not use it to mean "get along with."

✗ *How do you* **relate to** *your new psychiatrist?*
✓ *This point* **relates** *directly* **to** *my argument.*

## suppose to

Use "supposed to," or better, use "should" or "ought to."

## that/which

Use "that" when what follows restricts the meaning. Use "which" in a non-restrictive case.

*Here is the book* **that** *I told you about.* (not just any book, but a specific one)
*His fortune,* **which** *included stock certificates, bonds, and the first penny he had ever earned, was kept in an old shoebox under his bed.* (the words surrounded by commas supply incidental, non-restrictive information)

## their/there/they're

"Their" is possessive; "there" is an adverb or an expletive; "they're" is a contraction of "they are."

**There** *ought to be a law against* **their** *foolishness.* **They're** *asking for trouble.*

## try and

Replace this phrase with "try to."

*We must* **try to** *stop meeting like this.*

## unique

"Unique" means "one of a kind." It cannot be modified.

> ✗ Her sequined dress was **very unique**.
> ✓ Her sequined dress was **unique**.

## who's/whose

"Who's" is a contraction of "who is" or "who has"; "whose" is the possessive form.

> **Who's** been sleeping in my bed?
> **Whose** bed is this, anyway?

## -wise

Avoid this suffix.

> ✗ Timewise, the project is on schedule.
> ✓ The project is on schedule.

# Appendix — Answer Key

Suggested Answers to Exercises on Diction (Page 20)

## CHAPTER 3 EXERCISE 5A

1. I enjoy gambling, but I get annoyed when other people don't pay up.

2. Martin asked Darlene to have dinner with him, but she refused because he wanted to share the bill, and her payday wasn't until Friday.

3. Letter carriers are frequently bitten by unfriendly dogs.

4. The woman at the desk was extremely polite to the customers.

5. We were encouraged to avoid thinking about issues as if they were cut and dried.

6. People who were developmentally disabled were put in a special class.

7. Her mother is just about ready to go into a nursing home.

8. Having had polio, Allan sustained permanent damage to his muscles.

9. Women in the workforce must deal with many complicated demands on their time.

10. Single mothers are the main recipients of welfare.

## CHAPTER 3 EXERCISE 5B

1. Elizabeth has long been divorced.

2. Edith Piaf was an accomplished singer.

3. Dealing with a chronic ailment, people with arthritis suffer considerable pain upon arising.

4. Bettina uses a wheelchair.

5. Sandra Oh, the actor who appeared in *Oleanna*, is Korean.

6. He refused to go to a woman doctor.

7. She wanted to learn everything there was to know about the history of humankind.

8. Sheila Copps delivered a spirited address to Parliament.

9. She was a mother who worked outside the home.

10. Many First Nations people still live on the reserve.

## CHAPTER 16 EXERCISE A

Suggested Answers to Exercises on Comma Splices, Run-ons, and Fragments (Page 149)

1. The customer found the jalapeño peppers in the gumbo too hot, so he drank two pitchers of water during dinner.

2. The audience disliked the new play; they clearly felt that the director's talents did not lie in playwriting.

3. All the members of his family lacked inner resources; consequently, they sought constant stimulation and would never dream of picking up a book.

4. The children begged their father to buy a golden Labrador retriever, which soon became a much-loved part of the household and a symbol of domestic harmony.

5. The neighbours objected to the new apartment building development. City hall ignored their complaints and went ahead with the project anyway.

6. On the eighteenth floor, it can get rather windy; all the dust bunnies come out when there is a storm.

7. In Aristophanes' *Clouds*, a comic look at education, students destroy the university.

8. *The Dilbert Principle*, a non-fiction bestseller, explores how good employees get fired and bad employees get, ironically, promoted.

9. Correct.

10. Geoffrey grew a beard this past summer; it hid his double chin.

## EXERCISE B

1. Thelma bought a new convertible because the other one had been in an accident when she visited the Grand Canyon.

2. Poetry was Mei Ling's passion; cleaning house was her life.

3. Felix, Emily's cat, was demoralized by a raccoon. He was taken to the vet but released when the doctor failed to find a scratch on him.

4. Mimi distinguished herself when she wrote the entrance exam; she was probably the only candidate who wore a mink coat.

5. Jake liked souvenirs; he owned more fridge magnets, mugs, and rude postcards than anyone in the country.

6. Life in the residence upset Della. She missed her microwave, her privacy, and her cats.

7. Teresa didn't believe in career counsellors; instead, she made a lot of appointments with psychics.

8. Cindy Lou hated public transit. On her most recent bus trip she sat beside a fellow who laughed uncontrollably, for no apparent reason, every few minutes.

9. Mabel's experiences as an announcer on the local radio program made her wish that she could become a media celebrity.

10. Being excitable, Ginger, my terrier, greets guests by jumping up and down at the screen door.

## CHAPTER 16 EXERCISE A

Suggested Answers for Modifier Exercises (Page 152)

1. Travelling on the bus late at night, Jamie was alarmed by the sound of a passenger's maniacal laughter.

2. Living in the penthouse apartment in a high-rise, you may find it inconvenient when the power goes off.

3. When carrying a notebook computer, you feel that inspiration may strike at any time.

4. To accomplish everything on her gruelling schedule, she believes late nights, stamina, and many cups of coffee are essential.

5. Correct.

6. Recovering from last night's party, Doris and Russell found a quiet morning and a liquid breakfast seemed appealing.

7. Not pleased by the recent loss of his job, Tom developed a passion for *Dilbert* comic strips.

8. The retiring employees were interested only in the size of their pensions, not in the company's plans for a corporate takeover.

9. Not owning the latest computer equipment, Steven used handwritten notes for his contributions to the project.

10. A feasibility study determined that the easiest way to make money was to buy a parking lot.

## EXERCISE B

1. With a mop, Tessa killed the cockroach scurrying across the floor.

2. To impress your new boss, you should arrive on time.

3. Gabled and surrounded by beautiful trees and shrubs, the professor's home was declared a heritage property.

4. Taking the regional wine tour, Freddie saw the vineyard.

5. Correct.

6. As a taxpayer, I believe in the right to attend meetings at city hall.

7. After dropping a book on his toe, Geoffrey found his ability to get to class on time was severely affected.

8. Asleep at the wheel, the occupant of the car rolled it into the ditch; he escaped injury.

9. As a dedicated vegetarian, Giovanni buys only tomato sandwiches in the cafeteria.

10. Working out frequently in the gym, James improved his physique dramatically.

## CHAPTER 16 EXERCISE A

Suggested Answers to Pronoun Exercises (Page 156)

1. The menu says that someone whose allergies to certain foods present a problem may be specially accommodated by the chef.

2. As for me, I don't believe in relying on hypnosis for the answers to my problems. Hypnotists assume that all your problems are in your head.

3. To honour the occasion, the guests brought tacky shower presents for her and me (or us); we received them as graciously as possible, all the while wondering what we would do with all the kites and balloons.

4. All those whom we invited to the meeting had their own definite ideas about how to make more money.

5. All of the candidates for public office were vague about their platform; that way, they wouldn't have to back down later.

6. Emilio stepped on the lizard's tail, and the creature hissed at him.

7. The bestseller *Chicken Soup for the Soul* tells stories of how people overcame adversity and triumphed over their circumstances.

8. I was just as angry as she when I found out that the door to the classroom was locked; of course, she and I both had to find a custodian to let us in.

9. When a hockey player gets a penalty, everyone on the team suffers because of him (or her).

10. Just between you and me, he and his mother were shocked to discover that the school intended to close washrooms as a cost-cutting measure.

## EXERCISE B

1. Patricia had a wonderful idea for a business; her feasibility study said that what this country needs is a school for fools.

2. The tradition of the fool as the servant of powerful people exists in Shakespeare's work; Pat wondered if fools could not become a useful part of the modern economy as well.

3. The fool, according to Shakespeare, was often wise; he performed the useful social function of the moral conscience to the king.

4. If one were to imagine a chief executive officer in a large corporation, rather than a king, one might begin to appreciate how marketable this idea could become.

5. Graduates with sharp wits whose education has provided them with access to much-quoted wisdom would have an edge in the job market.

6. Correct.

7. The study which Pat wrote is liable to be considered a joke by some, but frankly, I think a fool might become a status symbol for the rich. A rich person would be hiring his or her own personal stand-up comedian.

8. Who do you suppose would be willing to admit that he wanted to be trained as a fool?

9. Each of the candidates for the course would be subjected to an audition to find out if he or she were able to make an audience laugh about human foibles.

10. Both Pat and I believe that there may be some stigma attached to the occupation of the fool; being funny, between you and me, is not really respectable, for some reason.

## CHAPTER 16 EXERCISE A

Suggested Answers to Subject and Verb Agreement Exercises (Page 160)

1. Sigrid, together with Kim, spends all the time painting, taking photographs, and watching videotapes of old movies.

2. Neither a borrower nor a lender is likely to befriend Brad after his latest entrepreneurial scheme.

3. The cost of the fax machine as well as the laser printer was prohibitive; the employees used the phone and wrote in pencil to save money.

4. There are a number of good reasons to buy a sofa bed: air mattresses are inconvenient and hardwood floors are hard on the back.

5. Defending family values and marketing children's services were Dustin's job as the new publicist.

6. The price of curtains seems extravagantly high, so his cousins decided to keep the windows bare.

7. Every single one of us has been nervous before a job interview, especially when we have been faced with a group of intimidating questioners.

8. Correct.

9. The vitamin supplement, along with the bee pollen, is meant to keep your energy levels high.

10. On the hard drive, unbeknownst to anyone, were a letter Leah had written to her brother and a diary of her innermost thoughts.

## EXERCISE B

1. At the bottom of Edwina's purse among her credit card receipts were a tiny bottle of vodka and a couple of straws.

2. A series of shocking crimes has been recently reported to the newspaper hot line.

3. Either Phil or Gwynneth makes hors d'oeuvres for the guests at the book club.

4. Spike, with his new tools and his powersaw, enjoys doing handy jobs around the house.

5. The fireworks on New Year's Eve were appreciated by all except the birds that inhabited the sycamore tree behind the house.

6. Neither Ross nor Barbra is available to answer the telephone at present.

7. The lack of jobs, along with an increase in consumer debt, has led to reduced spending.

8. Floor stripper, along with many cleaning solvents, is highly inflammable.

9. Travels to a previously unknown destination lead to creativity sometimes, as it did in the case of *Midnight in the Garden of Good and Evil* or *A Year in Provence*.

10. Jim's bad eating habits and unimaginative routine were his downfall.

## CHAPTER 16 EXERCISE A

Suggested Answers to Exercises on Colons and Semicolons (Page 163)

1. When her friends recommended hypnotism as a good way to break a bad habit, Briar was afraid she would wind up clucking like a chicken; however, she decided to give it a try.

2. The doctor assured her that people were not supposed to fall asleep; instead, they remained conscious throughout the entire session.

3. As she soon discovered, like her, many people were nervous at the thought of being hypnotized, mainly because they feared losing control.

4. Briar wanted to give up biting her nails, a habit which she considered unsightly, and she enlisted the hypnotist's help to do that.

5. In a post-hypnotic suggestion, the doctor warned her that her nails would now seem to have a dreadful, bitter taste that she would find repulsive.

6. He included that she would become gradually more interested in manicures and hand-care products.

7. In addition, he made this subliminal suggestion on a tape: that she would keep her hands busy by knitting compulsively whenever she felt an urge to chew her nails.

8. Briar knew that health insurance would probably not cover the cost of a hypnotist, but she felt she would benefit anyway: false nails are expensive; so are Band-Aids.

9. Now Briar's nails are as long as Barbra Streisand's; for some reason, she can't seem to stop knitting, however.

10. She doesn't cluck like a chicken, though now she can scratch like one.

---

## EXERCISE B

1. Commuting is a challenge to the strongest nerves: despite the weather, every day a driver must gear up for a journey that culminates in one rather unappealing thing: work.

2. People who commute regularly start to play mind games: some claim they have named all the trees along the route.

3. Correct.

4. Hazards like flat tires are common, so it is wise to carry a car phone or at least flares to alert other travellers.

5. If you are inclined, you may invest in motivational tapes or talking books, which will educate or, at any rate, distract you along the way.

6. Despite the temptation, commuters should not talk on the car phone, apply make-up, or comb their hair while driving.

7. Speeding tickets are another hazard: avoid a "heavy foot" when you feel pressed for time; if not, you will pay a fine, and your insurance rates will rise substantially.

8. Commuters should get a good night's sleep; when you are drowsy, you can stop for coffee at one of Canada's ubiquitous doughnut shops.

9. If you have to commute long distances, try to find a scenic route to dull the monotony occasionally: repetition is tedious and may lull you to sleep.

10. When you do get caught in traffic, however, relax, listen to the radio, and don't yell at other drivers.

---

## CHAPTER 16 EXERCISE A

Suggested Answers for Comma Exercises (Page 167)

1. Some cities in northern areas of Canada, like Saskatoon, have wide roads, something that allows for ease in snow removal.

2. As several members of the press noted, the radiator in Greg's office, admittedly old and in need of repair, emitted a strange odour and seemed unlikely to produce any heat.

3. Derk, her imaginary friend, surprised everyone by turning up at the dinner party with a bottle of ice wine, some panettone, and some catnip for the hostess's pets, to which he was allergic.

4. If Dave Broadfoot had six months to live, he would move to Dundas, Ontario, for he claims that six months there would feel like five years anywhere else.

5. When one of the new employees refused to evacuate the building during a fire drill, Regina, the new chief executive officer, was not impressed, so she decided to make an example of her.

6. Annie, the new director, expressed astonishment that the former house manager and the erstwhile publicist, both long since working at better jobs, would dare to set foot in the old theatre even in a spirit of nostalgia.

7. When he was told how well he was looking, Tyrone, shocked that anyone would be impressed by his appearance, backed up, held up one hand, smiled, and asked, "How many fingers am I holding up?" as if he were an optometrist.

8. Although the car was nicely warmed up and he was just about to cross the city limits, Bradley was alarmed that he had left Hilary behind, alone, asleep, and surrounded by paperwork in her office.

9. The most important job skill in the nineties is the ability to pack up the belongings in your office at a moment's notice.

10. Although Sean Connery, on his way to a nearby golf course, was rumoured to have been sighted on the elevator, neither Jocasta nor Clytemnestra managed to get a glimpse of him.

---

## EXERCISE B

1. Lawsuits that are launched by disgruntled employees, patients, and customers are often discussed in the papers lately, but some of us feel that revenge is a dish best eaten cold.

2. Selling Ray's house turned out to be an ordeal because the neighbours objected to the rezoning, and the termites put off prospective buyers.

3. For reasons she could not entirely fathom, the boss, perhaps jealous because of her financial success, told people that she made too much money; in fact, Delores began to wonder if that was the reason for her job loss.

4. If you are feeling bored, perhaps you should get Martha to teach you how to make gilt Easter eggs, decorate your house with wildflowers culled from the roadside, or give a party for seventy-five of your closest friends.

5. During the winter in cities like Victoria and Vancouver, snow can create problems; you see, hardly anyone keeps a shovel on hand.

6. Russians drink toasts to celebrate the simple joys of life; hence, Melanie discovered the joys of vodka when she stayed with a family in Minsk.

7. Emily was not superstitious in the slightest, so, against the best advice of her parents, she decided to name her first child Elektra.

8. Laughing hysterically, Malo imagined Aloha, his new puppy, dancing to amuse the tourists.

9. The server, claiming she had a hotel to run, refused to seat them indoors when it began to rain; as a result, the restaurant reviewer trashed the place severely in print.

10. Marie, who had always wanted to be a pirate, dreamed of starting a pirate school; in fact, she planned to teach courses while wearing an eye patch, swearing, and carrying a parrot on her shoulder.

## CHAPTER 16 EXERCISE A

Suggested Answers to Exercises on the Apostrophe (Page 171)

1. They went to Rodgers and Hammerstein's *The King and I* and Gershwin's *Porgy and Bess* as well as to more contemporary things like Jonathan Larson's *Rent* and Kander and Ebb's *Kiss of the Spider Woman*.

2. The department head compared the faculty's new programs of recruitment to Tim Horton's efforts to offer bagels as well as doughnuts.

3. A bagel's cost can't really compare to tuition's massive increases in a few years' time, however.

4. The actor's baby teeth were knocked out by the riot police; she was protesting the government's cutback of arts funding.

5. George's pets were a dog named Trouble and and a cat named Clio, after the muse of history: the dog's name was inaccurate since he was friendly and well behaved; the cat's name was unsuitable since history's a blank to her.

6. Gilbert's passion was garlic: the family's meal always featured its flavours; no week's groceries were complete without it, so his friends' reactions were to keep their distance.

7. Ellen's office was chaotic, and she seldom returned her clients' calls or paid her creditors' bills: she reasoned that she was right to ignore their requests; they, after all, ignored hers.

8. Scarlett was her father's daughter: she always went straight to the horse's mouth, and she thought she was the cat's meow.

9. The Beatles' claim to fame was their ability to influence not just music's directions, but young people's fashions and a whole generation's attitudes.

10. Company always regretted visits to the Strindbergs' house because the couple's arguments were so vehement, and their relatives' conversations were so distressing.

## EXERCISE B

1. After a hard day's negotiations, Theo's body refused to relax, and its tenseness prompted her husband to remind her of the worry dolls' powers; she put them on the bureau's surface, and she soon had a pleasant night's sleep.

2. Unimpressed by the city's magnificence even from the tallest building's outlook point, Cass responded with a yawn, captured forever in Alfred's photos of their trip.

3. It's unclear whether Denise's spouse's influence got her back on the job despite the cutbacks' impact, but some people suspect nepotism's influence.

4. Margaret Atwood's latest novel, *Alias Grace,* is taken from history's pages: she recounts a woman's story, and her responses to accusations of murder.

5. Joanne Kates's restaurant column in *The Globe and Mail* has its charms: she describes all the eateries' glories and flaws unflinchingly from a critic's perspective.

6. Margie Gillis's dancing is inspirational and energetic; its strength and beauty are well known to Canada's lovers of dance.

7. Charles Dickens's novels are best in their original forms. Some film directors' talents have enabled them to adapt the works into successful movies, but stage directors' ambitions are usually thwarted when Victorian writers' stories are turned into plays.

8. John Berendt's non-fiction work *Midnight in the Garden of Good and Evil* chronicles Savannah's citizens over several years' span.

9. Atom Egoyan's film work in movies like *Exotica* is complemented by his contributions to the Canadian Opera Company's repertoire in a recent production of Strauss's *Salome.*

10. Jane Austen's fame has spread in popular culture's circles in recent years: one notable success was Emma Thompson's screenplay of *Sense and Sensibility.*

## CHAPTER 17 EXERCISES

Suggested Answers to Exercises on Sentence Variation. (Page 175)

1. a. Wanting to catch her canary, Sadie chased it around the room with a guppy net, but the bird eluded her.
   b. Wishing to keep things neat and organized, Stacey insisted on keeping doors and windows shut both at work and at home and on folding plastic bags neatly into small squares before putting them away.
   c. Relishing his position as hall monitor, Steve walked through the school corridors with the confidence and attitude of a rooster, while boasting that his employment even improved his golf game.

2. a. Lonely and bored, Salvador put an ad in the personals column.
   b. A disaster, the ad attracted only other lonely, bored people, not socially adjusted ones.
   c. The phone call ended, Salvador sadly reported that it wasn't his dream date, but a social worker, asking if he had received his welfare cheque.

3. a. Although Gio and Millard tried to resist the temptation to buy a dog, they found Manfred, a gorgeous golden Labrador retriever, and bought him despite their misgivings.

b. Matilda swore off licorice because it stuck to her teeth and made her feel sick afterwards.

c. Whenever the nurse encouraged her patient, to coax him along, she always sang "Raindrops Keep Fallin' On My Head."

4. a. On the floor behind a heavy piece of furniture, she found the necklace.

b. Though Cecily and Sedgwick ran through the airport in a frenzy, they missed the plane.

c. Increasingly, it is reported that perpetrators of crime are children.

## CHAPTER 17 EXERCISE A

Suggested Answers to Exercises on Parallelism (Page 178)

1. Bernice went into hospital, received flowers and other tokens of affection, and enjoyed her physical complaints immensely.

2. Go to Hawaii for two weeks, or suffer unbearable jet lag after only a short stay.

3. On their visit to Vancouver, the twins went to Stanley Park, the art gallery, and a performance of "Bard on the Beach."

4. Being sound in mind and in body is essential when you make a legal document.

5. Not only did Evelyn send greeting cards to her brothers and sisters, but also she made sure they were given some of her famous homemade pies.

6. When reviewing a restaurant, you have to be mindful of service, ambience, and the quality of the food.

7. To get an MBA, you need lots of money to cover the high cost of tuition, experience or expertise in business, and great reserves of stamina.

8. Jane put on her long red gown, looked at herself hesitantly in the mirror, and remembered that she wanted to rent the video *Attack of the Killer Tomatoes!*

9. Mala missed her bus, spilled coffee all over herself, and vowed she would complain to the transit company.

10. Carlos loved Paris even though he suffered in its heat, could barely afford to buy a baguette, and lost ten pounds carrying his baggage.

## EXERCISE B

1. Edith and Henry waved at the tourists sailing by on the river, they enjoyed the scenery, and they chuckled to think that they would appear in people's home movies.

2. Kevin had an exhilarating swim, realized he couldn't find his clothes, and then spent hours wandering the beach in the nude, wishing he had worn sunscreen.

3. Nellie and Daphne disagreed not only about the colour of the carpet, but also about the placement of the paintings.

4. The therapist calmed Hugo's fears, made several suggestions, recorded a tape, and then asked for a credit card number.

5. Either Colm learns some manners on the telephone, or he will have to step down from his position in the department.

6. Either you could let Peggy and her basset hound into the living room, or you could go out on the front porch to chat.

7. Iain's job was as precarious as Rob's.

8. Neither the cabbage rolls and rice nor the borscht pleased Rex.

9. Emilio received a fur hat for his birthday, tried it on, and immediately began to imitate Bucky Beaver.

10. Accusations of favouritism will neither offend me, nor stop me from hiring my friends.

## CHAPTER 17 EXERCISE A

1. was spurred on — passive, hoped — active, would be entertained — passive

2. were eaten — passive, was said — passive

3. were adored — passive, were not enamoured — passive

4. were purchased — passive, was forced — passive, was revolted — passive

5. were shovelled — passive, were received — passive, had been inconvenienced — passive

6. were bombarded — passive, were stocked — passive, were not impressed — passive

7. was decided — passive, should be closed — passive, should be doubled — passive, should be laid off — passive

8. are documented — passive, has been shown — passive

9. has been well received — passive, sets — active

10. were written — passive

## EXERCISE B

1. was stolen — passive, left — active

2. were cancelled — passive, were stranded — passive, hit — active

3. sold — active, has benefited — passive

4. will be missed — passive, writes — active

5. will be fired — passive, is not improved — passive

6. has been renamed — passive

7. were collected — passive, [were] thrown — passive, [were] graded — passive, reached — active

8. was mounted — passive, were judged — passive, would have to be removed — passive

9. was damaged — passive, lost — active, rolled — active, was uninjured — passive

10. was attended — passive, were wined and dined — passive, were offered — passive

---

## CHAPTER 18 EXERCISE

Suggested Answers to Exercise on Wordiness (Page 185)

1. Now Ralph usually cycles to work, but he keeps his van running to transport his musical instruments.

2. Having to use electronic mail impressed Kay, though she still preferred remaining physically close to loved ones.

3. Sandra, in my estimate, is not a capable hairdresser, and I will have to find another.

4. Piglet reported to Winnie that the broken balloon was small and red.

5. Cedric's exhibition at the art gallery used household furniture to explore the decline of domestic values; I cannot judge whether the work is innovative.

6. Steve planned to immortalize his roommates: he believed that the story of Bobby, Luciano, and Bruce would be an entertaining situation comedy, although he doubted whether it would be believable.

7. Carmelina purchased this print at the mall after she haggled with the salesclerk over its price.

8. That we cannot appreciate his jokes is unimportant because we are responsible for inviting him; we must tolerate him.

9. A married woman who planned to have children, Fiona decided to take her husband's last name.

10. Students wishing to attain high marks forget that underpaid teachers might consent if compensated.

# Index

# Reader Reply Card

We are interested in your reaction to *Fit to Print: The Canadian Student's Guide to Essay Writing,* Fourth Edition by Joanne Buckley. You can help us to improve this book in future editions by completing this questionnaire.

1. What was your reason for using this book?

   ☐ university course    ☐ college course    ☐ continuing education course
   ☐ professional         ☐ personal      ☐ other _____
       development        interest       _____

2. If you are a student, please identify your school and the course in which you used this book.

3. Which chapters or parts of this book did you use? Which did you omit?

4. What did you like best about this book? What did you like least?

5. Please identify any topics you think should be added to future editions.

6. Please add any comments or suggestions.

7. May we contact you for further information?

   Name: _____

   Address: _____

   _____

   Phone: _____

(fold here and tape shut)

---

0116870399-M8Z4X6-BR01

Larry Gillevet
Director of Product Development
HARCOURT BRACE & COMPANY, CANADA
55 HORNER AVENUE
TORONTO, ONTARIO
M8Z 9Z9